FIRE ENGINES

FIRE ENGINES

Peter Henshaw

CHARTWELL
BOOKS, INC.

Published in 2009 by
CHARTWELL BOOKS, INC.
A division of BOOK SALES, INC.
276 Fifth Avenue
Suite 206
New York
NY 10001
USA

**Copyright © 2009 Regency
House Publishing Limited**
The Red House
84 High Street
Buntingford, Hertfordshire
SG9 9AJ, UK

For all editorial enquiries, please contact
Regency House Publishing at
www.regencyhousepublishing.com

ISBN-13: 978-0-7858-2405-3

ISBN-10: 0-7858-2405-7

Printed in China

CONTENTS

INTRODUCTION

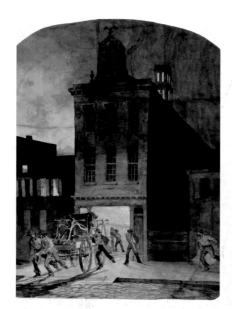

terrifying force, capable of destroying life, property, the environment and everything that civilization holds dear.

Fire was one of the four classical elements in ancient Greek philosophy, along with air, water and earth, and was commonly associated with energy,

FAR LEFT: Early Philadelphia firefighters answer a call in around 1857.

BELOW: A horse-drawn steam pump attends the San Francisco Ferry Building.

OPPOSITE: A fire crew pose in front of a well-equipped Alexandria, Virginia, fire station.

Since the time that man first learned to make fire, turning it to his own advantage to provide heat, light and a means of cooking food, there have been occasions when fire has occurred spontaneously, at the wrong time and in the wrong place. The harnessing of this simple chemical reaction was undoubtedly a step change in the evolution of the human race that brought huge benefits, yet fire could, and still can, be a disastrous and

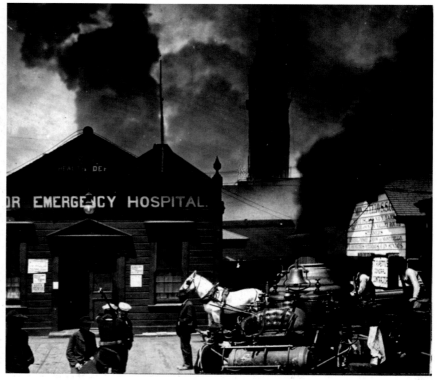

FIRE ENGINES

assertiveness, and passion. In Greek mythology, it was Prometheus the Titan who decided to steal fire from Zeus and

OPPOSITE: A smartly appointed horse-drawn steamer at York, Pennsylvania.

ABOVE: San Francisco's earthquake of 1906 presented a great challenge for firefighters.

give it to mortals for their own use. Zeus seems to have been disproportionately angry at the crime, perhaps because he was keeping this civilizing element from man, and punished Prometheus by having him bound to a rock while a great eagle ate his liver, which regenerated the next day so that the punishment could be

endlessly repeated. But it is Prometheus, nevertheless, who is credited with bringing this geat gift to mankind, which may be regarded as something of a mixed blessing, being both life-enhancing and destructive at the same time.

Firefighting is the act of extinguishing a destructive fire. A fire

INTRODUCTION

starts when a flammable and/or a combustible material with an adequate supply of oxygen or another oxidizer is subjected to sufficient heat that will enable it to sustain a chain reaction, commonly called the fire tetrahedron.

Fire cannot exist without all of these elements being present, but it can be extinguished by removing any one element of the tetrahedron. Extinguishing a fire using water acts by removing the heat from the fuel faster

BELOW: Testing early petrol pumpers in New York.

OPPOSITE & PAGE 14: A 1914 British Dennis fire engine.

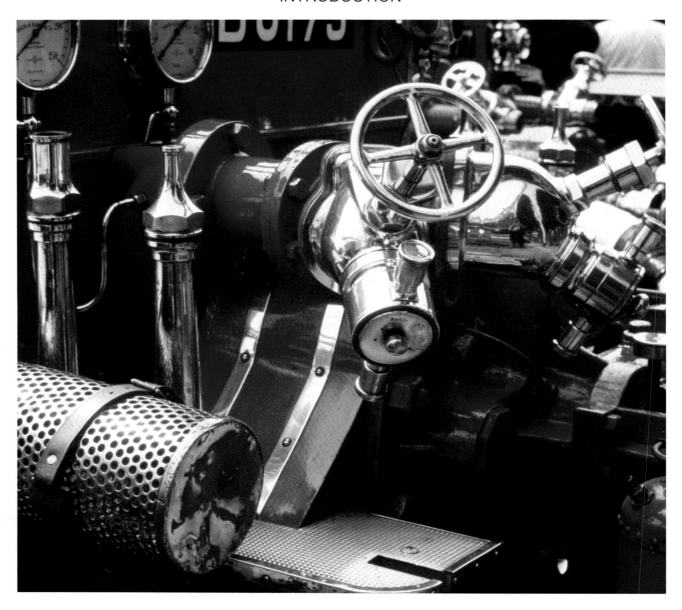

FIRE ENGINES

than combustion can generate it, while the application of carbon dioxide is intended primarily to starve the fire of oxygen. A wildfire may be fought by starting smaller fires in advance of the main blaze, which will deprive it of fuel, while other gaseous suppression agents, such as halon, which is an unreactive compound of carbon with bromine and other halogens, also HFC-227, interfere with the chemical reaction itself.

BELOW: A 1913 Commer fire engine, with four-cylinder 3.8-litre engine.

There is evidence that organized firefighting, albeit in a primitive form, existed within the Roman Empire as early as 300 BC. Later, Augustus, the first Roman emperoror, appointed the

ABOVE: The Clayton, New Jersey Fire Department, pictured in around 1920.

RIGHT: Poor brakes and roadholding often led to accidents when on duty.

OPPOSITE: Ever greater attention was given to firefighting following San Francisco's 1906 earthquake.

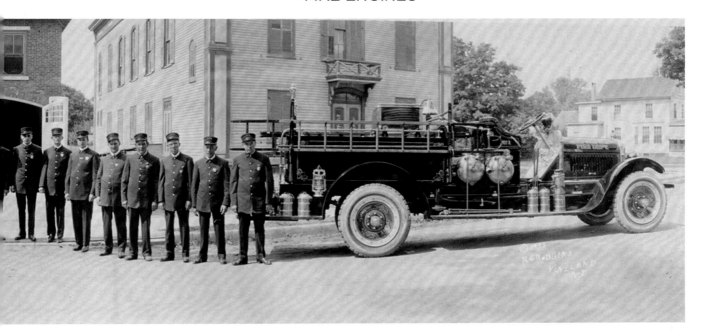

Corps of Vigiles, more properly the
Vigiles Urbani ('watchmen of the city'),
to be the firefighters and policemen of
ancient Rome. Every cohort was
equipped with standard firefighting
equipment. The *sipho*, or fire engine,
was pulled by horses and consisted of a
large double-action pump that was
partially submerged in a reservoir of
water. The *vigiles* designated as *aquarii*,
or water-carriers, needed to know
where water was located, and human
chains were formed to pass buckets of
water to the fire. Attempts were also

RIGHT: A magnificent American LaFrance fire engine from the 1920s.

BELOW: Skill is needed to operate pump controls.

made to smother fire, by covering it with quilts (*centones*) soaked in water, and there is evidence that a vinegar-based substance, known as *acetum*, was used to subdue it. Sometimes, the best way of preventing the spread of flames

FIRE ENGINES

OPPOSITE: The task of driving an early engine was a complex job.

BELOW: Multiple ignition systems were used to ensure reliability.

was to tear down burning buildings using hooks and levers, while cushions and mattresses would be spread out to soften the landing of people jumping from the upper storeys of tall buildings.

For centuries after the Romans, firefighting was no more sophisticated, and as towns grew in size and density, with their flammable wooden buildings squeezed together in close proximity,

FIRE ENGINES

LEFT: Early firefighters were exposed to the elements in all kinds of weather. This is a New Zealand fire engine from the 1920s.

ABOVE: The klaxon siren is clearly visible.

the consequences of major fires became all the more catastrophic, the Great Fire of London being one among many examples. The disaster occurred in 1666, when a baker's shop in London's

FIRE ENGINES

LEFT: A workmanlike fire engine once in use in County Galway, Ireland.

BELOW: Bells were the precursors of sirens.

Pudding Lane caught fire and the blaze spread quickly through the neighbouring medieval houses. It burned fiercely for five days, spreading through the city's streets and destroyed 3,000 houses and 87 churches.

Prior to London's Great Fire, firefighting measures had been minimal, and there was little attempt to organize firefighting on a municipal

INTRODUCTION

scale after it, although hand pumps had begun to appear. These were crude devices, operated by means of levers connected to pistons in pump barrels, but they could still deliver more water, and with greater force, than a bucket

ABOVE: Dennis was one of the English pioneers where firefighting was concerned.

LEFT: A legendary Green Goddess, the colloquial name for the Bedford RLHZ Self-Propelled Pump.

OPPOSITE: Vintage New Zealand appliances.

INTRODUCTION

BELOW: Cabs were still ten years away when this open 1930s English fire engine was in active duty.

RIGHT: A Ford-based appliance used by Royal Ordnance munition factories in Britain during the Second World War.

chain. Hand pumps could also be made portable, by mounting them on wheeled chassis that could be pulled to the site of a fire where, operated by four or five men, a stream of water could be projected 40ft (12m) into the air.

Such hand pumps, of course, delivering water from a tub or cistern, still had to be filled by bucket. In 1672, the Dutch engineer Jan van der Heiden invented a pump that could draw water from a pond or river by suction, and deliver it to the fire by means of a leather hose. Another improvement was to have two handles, one on each side, which not only allowed 'all hands to the pump', that had previously applied to seafarers, but also meant that there were effectively two pumps delivering a continuous stream of water rather than a series of ineffectual squirts.

In England, Richard Newsham (d. 1743) was a prolific maker of hand pumps, and at one point offered six

LEFT: This old Mercedes is still in use in its native land.

ABOVE: A vintage Dodge from the Georgetown Fire Department.

ABOVE: A cab-forward appliance at work in Springfield in 1967.

RIGHT: Another classic Ford appliance.

different sizes that delivered from 30 gallons per minute (gpm) up to 170gpm.

AMERICAN LAFRANCE:
A HOUSEHOLD NAME

*F*ew *names are better known in the world of fire engines than that of American LaFrance. Once the longest-established and longest-lived of all such American manufacturers, it dominated the industry for decades until January 2008, when its fate lay in the balance, and it closed up shop a few months later.*

American LaFrance's roots lay in the 19th century, the company having been the result of a merger between two big players: the American Fire Engine Company, that was formed in 1891, and which was itself the result of a merger between a number of steam engine manufacturers, and

Truckson LaFrance, founded in 1872 (the name was actually Hyenveux, thought to be unpronouncable by English-speakers, hence the change to LaFrance).

LaFrance quickly earned a good reputation for building fine hand and steam pumps, and in 1901 merged with its chief rival – the American Fire Engine Company, plus a number of others – as the International Fire Engine Company. With production consolidated at the LaFrance works in Elmira, New York, it was clear from the start who was the senior partner, which was confirmed in 1904 when the name was changed to American LaFrance. (By way of explanation,

Ward LaFrance, despite the name and the fact that it was also based in Elmira and was started by a member of the same family, had no connection with American LaFrance, and was, in fact, a serious rival.)

But American LaFrance was no pioneer when it came to petrol-powered fire engines, even though it delivered a petrol-driven chemical appliance to the Boston Fire Department in 1907, and two more combination chemical/hose wagons in 1909; but it wasn't until 1910 that the machine listed on the official American LaFrance register as Number One was delivered. This was a Type 5 combination chemical/hose engine, based on a four-cylinder Simplex chassis, with which

American LaFrance appeared to have found its feet, and 20 more were built that same year.

In 1911, the company was offering pumpers in two sizes, the 500-gpm Type 10 and 750-gpm Type 12, both with rotary-gear pumps. The same year, the fire department at Savannah, Georgia, became the first to be fully motorized in the USA, its fleet having come entirely from American LaFrance. The company built its last steam pump in 1914, though it continued to service the old steamers well into the 1920s. Moreover, the fact that it had finally become motorized seems to have done American LaFrance a power of good, for nearly 2,000 appliances were sold between 1910 and 1917, which was more than all the other major US manufacturers put together were able to achieve.

One of the reasons for its success was the very wide range of models. In the 1920s, hundreds of Model T Fords were being converted into light fire engines by the addition of American LaFrance equipment, a typical example of this being two 25-gallon chemical tanks, 150ft (46m) of hose, a fire extinguisher, a 16-ft (5-m) ladder, lanterns, an axe, crowbar and the essential bell. The Type 75 of the mid-1920s was more like a full-sized fire engine, with a six-cylinder T-head engine and 750-gpm pump, but it was still relatively light and manoeuvrable and was highly successful.

At the same time, American LaFrance had been producing some of the most powerful machines on the market, including, as early as 1916, a pumper of 1000gpm, and ever more powerful pumpers followed in the next two decades, partly to cope with America's burgeoning skyscrapers, and the company had a 3000-gpm machine in its catalogue by 1937.

Technology had also moved on, and the Master Series (or Type 200), announced in 1929, had four-wheel brakes, left-hand steering and an automatic cooling system. Power came from a 140-hp (104.4-kW) six-cylinder T-head engine, and the company designed and produced its own 240-hp (179-kW) V12 from 1931, and would go on to produce buses,

trucks and generators as well as fire engines. American LaFrance made a move towards diversification into trucks and other lines at this time, none of which was really successful, for its heart seemed to remain with fire equipment.

After the Second World War, the company pioneered a cab-forward design with the distinctive 700 Series. It continued to be a leading maker of aerial ladders, while being taken over by A-T-O Incorporated, in 1966, placed it in the same stable as the Snorkel Fire Equipment company, creating a strong lineup of appliances. Custom-built chassis were introduced in 1973, but the company also continued to offer commercial chassis, notably the budget-priced Pioneer line in the 1990s. On 25 July 2008, the company re-emerged from bankruptcy with a revised business plan which will hopefully allow it to continue though possibly in a different form.

CHAPTER ONE
STEAMERS, PUMPERS, LADDERS & SNORKELS

While the technology of firefighting may have been creeping forward, its organization, up until the early 19th century, was still haphazard. Many of the early brigades in Europe and North America had been set up by insurance companies, which of course stood to lose in the event of clients' property simply being left to burn down. Firefighters, moreover, were paid only to tackle the fires in buildings insured by their bosses, rather than those of rival companies, the primary aim of both being to save property rather than human lives.

BELOW LEFT: Supercharging and turbocharging delivers extra power.

OPPOSITE: International Harvester chassis have been used for fire engines.

Sometimes rivalries would spring up between volunteer brigades, which in North America led to ugly scenes when they attempted to fight the same fires, not to mention, on occasions, each other. Eventually, the insurance companies came to the conclusion that they all stood to gain by co-operating with one another, and more efficient firefighting was the result. In 1866, the Metropolitan Fire Brigade was launched in London, this being one of the first paid for out of public funds, and which was as concerned with saving lives as it was with preserving bricks and mortar.

THE STEAM REVOLUTION
By this time, steam power had become well-established as a means of powering pumps, and with the near-universal adoption of steam in industry and on

the railroads, it was not long before steam-powered fire engines were appearing out on the streets. The first had been built by John Braithwaite

(1797–1870) and John Ericsson in London in 1829. Mounted on a four-wheeled wagon, and designed for horse traction, it weighed a little over

5,000lbs (2270kg), this being about twice as much as an equivalent hand pump. It could raise steam from cold in 13 minutes, and was able to pump

150gpm to a height of 90ft (27m). But the London Fire Brigade refused to use it, although Braithwaite was able to sell another steamer to the Liverpool fire service in 1831.

The first American experiment was conducted in New York in 1840 by a coalition of insurance companies. English-born Paul Rapsey Hodge took on the assignment, and as an ex-railway engineer designed a massive machine that had more in common with a locomotive than any road vehicle. Christened *Exterminator*, it was over 13-ft (4-m) long and weighed more than 14,000lbs (6350kg), with large wrought-iron drive wheels that were jacked up to operate as flywheels at the scene of the fire.

Exterminator was demonstrated to the New York public in 1841, and proved itself able to shoot a stream of water 166ft (50m) into the air. Unfortunately, it took half an hour to get up a sufficient head of steam, and although it was self-propelled, its prodigious weight meant that the ponderous beast was unable to answer emergency calls with lightning speed. No one was impressed, and *Exterminator* ended up working as a stationary engine for a box-maker.

Excessive weight would always be the enemy of early steam power when the engine was expected to be self-propelled, but a more effective device was a steam-powered pump, light enough to be drawn by horses or even by the firefighters themselves. This time it was Cincinnati which saw one such early experiment, and it was also a graphic illustration of the superiority of steam over hand-pumping. Partners Alexander Latta and Abel Shawk built a steam pump that could shoot water 130ft (40m) into the air through 350ft (117m) of hosepipe, and because Shawk had devised a copper coil that dramatically cut the waiting time, it also took only five minutes to raise the steam.

The city council was so impressed that it commissioned Latta and Shawk to build another engine. Named *Uncle Joe Ross*, in honour of the council's leader, this was far more of a heavyweight, which at 22,000lbs (9980kg) needed a team of four horses to haul it, though it was also partially self-propelled. On 1 January 1853, it was pitted against the most powerful hand pump in the city in order to prove the new-fangled device. The volunteers and their hand pump got to the site first, and were already pumping hard by the time the steamer arrived. But once *Uncle Joe* finally got going, it was able to spray water 225ft (69m) into the air and keep going, whereas the exhausted hand-pumpers had to give up after half an hour.

For many brigades, steamers remained too heavy, expensive and slow throughout most of the 19th century, but successful self-propelled steamers eventually appeared, such as Merryweather's Fire King, which was supplied to several English brigades. Oil-fired, it came in six sizes, from 300 to 1000gpm, the steam engine pushing it along at 20–30mph (32–48km/h). Meanwhile, in New Hampshire in the USA, the Manchester Locomotive Works had become famous for its self-propelled steamers, which from 1874 had the advanced feature of a differential, which was of great help when cornering.

Driving one of these machines was still a two-man operation: an engineer stood at the rear to operate the throttle, and the driver sat in front, in charge of the brakes and a huge, vertical steering wheel. With two men doing the driving, one of whom could not easily see what was coming, accidents were inevitable.

FIRE ENGINES

At a time when fire engines were becoming heavier and faster, the idea of a pedal-powered appliance may seem laughable today, but a bicycle fire engine was seriously proposed in the late 19th century. The invention of the safety cycle in 1887 led to a bicycling craze, and in 1899 the fire commissioner of Washington, DC proposed sending a bicycle-mounted firefighter onto the streets ahead of the main engine, with a fire extinguisher strapped to his back. In Paris, the idea went still further, and a four-man quadricycle appeared, complete with pump and hose reel, which, on arrival at the fire, could be transformed into a pedal-powered pump.

Despite such minimalist ideas, and although many volunteer brigades retained the simpler, cheaper hand pumps, no one doubted the ultimate supremacy of steam, and a horse-drawn steam pump became the standard municipal fire engine in the late 19th century. Early steamers could manage only 200gpm, but as the technology improved and competition between rival manufacturers intensified, rates of up to 500gpm were achieved. Merryweather (see pages 80–81) and Shand Mason were the leading makes

in England, offering a variety of different formats. Merryweather's 'Greenwich Gem' steamer, for example, was available in four sizes, from 225 to 500gpm, at a cost of £400 to £550 with all tools and hoses supplied.

All of these were coal-fired, though London's Metropolitan Fire Brigade made the change to oil-fired steamers in 1900. Coal-fired machines could be converted to oil for as little as £35, with a new burner that used steam from the boiler to spray oil into the furnace, and engines could carry up to three hours' supply of oil, this being a lighter and longer-lasting fuel than coal. The steamer may have been under threat from the internal combustion engine, but some were still working on its improvement. Merryweather attached a cylinder of compressed carbon dioxide to the boiler, which could be used to increase the draught to the fire; Shand Mason had the engineer wind a handle on the way to a fire, which turned a fan in the funnel to increase draught, the company claiming 100lb (450kg) of steam pressure from cold in as little as five minutes.

PETROL VS ELECTRIC POWER

Although steam-propelled fire engines

existed, most were still hauled by horses, which presented problems of their own. Horses had to be bought and trained; they needed fodder, shoeing and veterinary care, which all cost money, while fodder also needed to be stored. In short, horses were expensive and labour-intensive.

Not that steam was without drawbacks of its own. Boiler explosions were rare, but they did sometimes occur, and steamers carried only enough coal for a run of 30 minutes or so, which meant that a horse-drawn tender was also required. Steamers were themselves a fire risk, and it was not unknown for sparks from a steamer to set fire to hedges and hayricks as it dashed towards the main conflagration. And while we may have a somewhat romantic view of steam power today, the 19th-century reality was noisy, smoky, hot and generally unpleasant. Fortunately, the next step in the development of the fire engine was just around the corner.

But at the dawn of the 20th century it was still unclear what form this would take, for in 1900, both petrol and electric power appeared equally attractive. Even steam wasn't quite done for yet, for the invention of the

STEAMERS, PUMPERS, LADDERS & SNORKELS

LEFT: A 1936 Leyland-Metz appliance.

OPPOSITE: An early Dennis with crew cab.

flash boiler in 1889 had allowed the development of lightweight, high-pressure steam engines that started relatively quickly from cold. Steamers were easier and cheaper to make than petrol engines, not to mention easier to drive, in that they could not stall and needed fewer gear changes. But as petrol engines became more powerful and reliable, these advantages began to fade away, and steam was effectively obsolete as an alternative by 1905.

Electric power, of course, had the starting problems of neither, being clean, quiet and extremely easy to operate. By 1900, all-electric fire engines were in operation in Paris, Hannover and Vienna, while in Springfield, Massachusetts, an electric Knox combination wagon was in use in 1914. The Parisian engine was equipped with a pump, hook and ladder, all powered by 1,300lbs (590kg) of batteries, and one charge allowed the engine to travel up to 35 miles (56km) at an average speed of 12mph (19km/h), which doesn't sound much but was sufficient for its time. The

DENNIS: THE SURVIVOR

*D*ennis deserves to be called a survivor. Of the three leading British manufacturers, the others being Leyland and Merryweather, only this company is still active in the 21st century, 100 years after building its first fire engine. Brothers John and Raymond Dennis went into business in the 1890s, rapidly making the transition from bicycles to motorized tricycles and quadricycles, then to cars, buses, vans and lorries, with the first Dennis fire engine appearing in 1908.

Dennis fire trucks were exported all over the world, and the company produced thousands of vehicles of all types during both World Wars, its much respected F-series having been launched after the Second World War. The F1, for example, was a favourite of fire brigades in rural Ireland, where its narrow width enabled it to access narrow lanes. The first forward-control Dennis was the F7 from 1949, while the F8 was offered right through the 1950s. Many of these were built to the requirements of individual brigades, but the standard F8 was powered by a 4.25-litre Rolls-Royce six-cylinder engine of 122bhp, with a rear-mounted pump delivering 500gpm.

But Dennis was severely affected by competition in the 1960s and was taken over by Hestair in 1972. Renamed Hestair Dennis, the company concentrated on exports, winning a Queen's Award for Export in 1977. It later re-entered the UK home market successfully, and in 1991 moved to a new factory. It later closed, but the name was revived in John Dennis Coachbuilders, which has regained the UK market leadership and offers the Sabre multi-purpose fire engine and the Dagger compact fire tender, as well as appliances based on chassis by Volvo, MAN, Mercedes and Scania.

French engine carried a 100-gallon water tank, and the pump was driven by a basic power take-off.

The great disadvantage of electric vehicles, then as now, was their restricted range. Thirty-five miles was sufficient to answer calls within a city, but recharging took many hours. The batteries also needed to be periodically replaced, they were not cheap, and they were also very heavy.

A potential solution was to combine the benefits of petrol and electricity in what we would now call a hybrid vehicle, and Tilling-Stevens in the UK produced some of these petrol-electric chassis. The petrol engine powered a generator, which in turn drove the wheels, giving the advantages of electric power without the short range. The company designed a petrol-electric fire engine in 1919, in which the dynamo was able to drive either the wheels or a turbine pump. Having an electric pump, interestingly, meant that it could be demounted from the engine and wheeled to wherever it was required, connected to the dynamo via a cable.

LEFT & OPPOSITE: A 1936 Bedford Merryweather.

FIRE ENGINES

But even as Tilling-Stevens was perfecting its petrol-electric technology, time was already running out for these early electrics. By then, petrol had become the motive power of choice for fire engines, offering reliability and a compact, relatively lightweight fuel source. Some of the earliest petrol-powered fire engines were at work in Germany, the country that pioneered the petrol power unit, and a few fire departments were using them as early as 1901. In fact, Daimler had built a horse-drawn appliance with a petrol-powered pump back in 1888. An example of the early petrol-driven engine was the Magirus, with its twin-cylinder Daimler unit producing up to 15hp (11.2kW), and propelling the four-man appliance up to 12mph. Like the steamers, it carried both driver and engineer, each with their own steering and brakes, and also came with a three-cylinder pump that delivered 200gpm.

In Britain, too, where some pioneering fire brigades used petrol appliances, a first-aid tender, based on a Bijou car, was delivered in September 1901. In March 1903, a Daimler-chassised appliance was delivered to the town of Leamington Spa, in Warwickshire, England, complete with

chemical engine, hose, and a 30-ft (9-m) wheeled escape. Later that same year, Merryweather, which would build fire engines for 70 years, built a combination or multi-purpose appliance with a petrol-engined escape, a compressed-air fire engine following

in 1905, while the company had also supplied the world's first single-engined appliance to Baron de Rothschild's estate in France the previous year.

Uncharacteristically, American fire departments were slow to exploit the potential of petrol, though New York

bought two Mercedes cars for chiefs to use in 1904, while two years later, the USA's first petrol fire engine went into service with the Radnor Fire Company of Wayne, Pennsylvania. It was built by

A Morris Minor factory fire engine.

FIRE ENGINES

the Waterous Engine Works of St. Paul, Minnesota, a well-established company that made steam pumpers with two separate motors, one to drive the appliance, the other to run the rear-mounted 300-gpm pump. The second Waterous petrol appliance had only one engine, which drove both wheels and pump. Waterous has long since ceased to make complete appliances, but over 100 years later it remains one of the leading makers of pumps.

Petrol vehicles gave a good account of themselves during the San Francisco earthquake of 1906, and the acting fire chief of the city commandeered 200 private cars to help in the rescue effort. 'I was sceptical about the automobile previous to the disaster,' he reported, 'but now give it my hearty endorsement.' Even so, it would be another three years before New York bought its first motorized fire appliance, this being a high-pressure hose wagon from Knox, which was equipped with a fixed turret nozzle and an acetylene searchlight. It could also top 30mph (48km/h), which illustrates how rapidly petrol power was beginning to develop.

Merryweather, one of the big three British makers of fire engines, has already been mentioned, and its US equivalent was undoubtedly American LaFrance, another pioneer of the industry. It was formed by merger in 1901 between the American Fire Engine and the LaFrance Fire Engine Companies, building its first petrol-powered appliance six years later, although 'Number 1', based on a Simplex chassis, didn't appear until 1910. By 1911, the company was offering pumpers that were combination chemical/hose carts and straight chemical engines.

Chemical engines, incidentally, were an attempt to eliminate pumps, and carried a solution of bicarbonate of soda and water rather than water alone. Sulphuric acid was released from a bottle within the tank at the fire scene, the subsequent chemical reaction forcing the water out under gas pressure, rather like a giant soda syphon. A chemical engine was able to deliver a jet of water for anything up to 15 minutes and, with its attendant power source, needed no pump. The disadvantage, however, was that, once set in motion, the chemical reaction could not be stopped. But its plus points meant that many saw service in the late 19th century and into the first decade of the next. A more convenient alternative was compressed-air delivery, and Shand Mason built such a machine in 1898. This had a cylinder of compressed air that could be turned on or off at will to deliver a water jet, but this too was soon superseded by the convenience of petrol-powered pumps.

DIFFERENT STROKES

Although it was clear that petrol was the answer where fire engines were concerned, the exact form taken by the vehicles varied. Motorcycle and sidecar outfits offered some advantages for quick response, added to which was their ability to be on the scene before the main engine. Merryweather produced the first of these in 1910, and there were several more examples throughout the 1920s and '30s. Dunford & Elliot, for example, unveiled the Dunelt-XLCR in 1924 based, as the name suggests, on a Dunelt motorcycle, which was equipped with a 25-gallon chemical set-up, 25ft (8m) of hose, three 3-gallon 'Sprafoam' extinguishers, a small CTC extinguisher, and a 12-ft (4-m) ladder. In 1932 Dennis, by then well-established in the industry, produced a similar outfit based on a BSA motorcycle.

The ubiquitous Ford Model T, in that it was one step up from a sidecar combination, was another candidate ripe for conversion. It was a relatively simple job to fit a small pump or chemical pump to a Model T, and many small-town mechanics were able to do the job. American LaFrance, among others, offered its own conversion on the Model T chassis, and the Model TT truck became a favourite with smaller, more rural fire departments.

The petrol revolution that gathered pace in the early 20th century presented many fire chiefs with a serious problem. Most still used reliable, well-made steam pumpers that were still in the prime of life, and to scrap these in favour of new petrol fire engines would have been prohibitively expensive. But help was at hand, in that once a petrol tractor unit had been bought, it could be hitched up to an existing steamer, delivering speed and power while squeezing a few more years of work out of the old machinery. As for the fire

RIGHT: A Ford light truck-based fire engine.

PAGES 48–49: A Dennis pumper used by the New Zealand Fire Service.

FIRE ENGINES

horses, they were retired in their thousands, often not without regret.

Some of the early tractors, such as those built by Couple Gear in the USA, were electric, but the future lay in petrol, a pioneer of which was John Walter Christie, who introduced his two-wheeled, transverse-engine design in 1912, this being a tough and reliable tractor that could pull up to 12 tons; the Fire Department City of New York (FDNY) would buy 300 of these, which was about half the total production. American LaFrance made tractors, too, starting with the Type 17 in the same

LEFT: A Magirus-Deutz with an aerial ladder.

BELOW: A Tatra four-cylinder appliance of 1932.

year as that of the Christie. This was a four-wheeler, powered by a six-cylinder 105-hp (78.3-kW) engine, with a three-speed transmission and chain drive. It was soon joined by the two-wheeled Type 31, offered in 75-hp (55.9-kW) four-cylinder or 105-hp six-cylinder forms, which remained in production right up to 1929.

Most tractors were based on this same format, though Knox-Martin

A roofless American LaFrance fire engine in service with the Vero Beach Fire Department, Florida.

offered a three-wheeled alternative from 1909, its single front wheel steering via a long column extended over the hood. It looked odd, but this 40-hp (29.8-kW) trike could reach 30mph (48km/h) and turn through 90 degrees, though not at the same time, making it highly manoeuvrable. But by the late 1920s, the tractor era was rapidly drawing to a close, simply because the sturdy steamers were finally wearing out, giving fire departments and brigades the chance to purchase completely new appliances.

REACH FOR THE SKY

Tractors not only towed pumpers, but were the means by which aerial, or turntable, ladders were also hauled to the scene. Daniel D. Hayes, the chief mechanic of the San Francisco Fire Department, is thought to have been the first builder of a successful turntable ladder. He reasoned that being able to manoeuvre a ladder in any direction and at any angle was far quicker and easier than trying to manhandle the entire appliance into place. His wooden aerial ladder,

patented in 1868, was raised by means of a worm gear, and could reach 85ft (26m) when 50–60ft had been the previous norm. It was a step forward, but the horses first had to be unhitched, and the hefty ladder needed five or six firefighters to turn the lifting handle. This bottleneck, created when raising the ladder, would be the subject of development, but it would be decades before the modern hydraulic aerial ladder became widespread.

The Babcock, first demonstrated in 1886 and built by the Fire Extinguishing Manufacturing Company, was more easily raised by vertical worm screws, which meant that two firefighters could raise it with one hand crank each. But a real pointer to the future came only a couple of years later, when Chief E.F. Dahill, of New Bedford, Massachusetts, devised a system using compressed air, and the Dahill Air Hoist was soon being offered by most makers of aerial ladders in the USA.

An alternative was manual spring-assist, patented by Seagrave in 1902. This used twin lifting springs to help raise the main part of the ladder, which was then extended by means of conventional hand cranks. This was a

real step forward, and many manufacturers began offering spring-assisted aerials in the early 20th century. The one sold by American LaFrance, from 1904, featured an hydraulic cylinder to control the ladder's extension, all-hydraulic operation being, of course, still some way off.

In England, Merryweather offered a range of variations on the theme, with ladders between 60 and 120ft (18 and 36.5m) powered by carbon dioxide gas, compressed air, or a petrol engine mounted on the turntable, although

BELOW: There are extended four-door cabs on these Mitsubishi-based engines.

RIGHT: A light-duty pumper serves this volunteer brigade in New Zealand.

hand-cranking for ladders up to 80ft (24m) was still available. Some Merryweather engines also used the road engine to raise and extend the ladder, the system doing both jobs at the same time while the turntable was hand-cranked. This appliance was advertised in 1921, though the following year Morris-Magirus

delivered an appliance to the Glasgow Fire Brigade, the petrol engine of which drove the turntable as well, allowing the ladder to be turned, raised and extended simultaneously using the same power source.

Ladders are usually considered to be rescue devices, though more often they were convenient platforms from which to direct water onto tall buildings. Water towers were designed purely for the latter purpose, and as the USA led the world in high-rise buildings in the late 19th and early 20th centuries, this is where development was concentrated.

The Portable Stand-Pipe or Water Tower was the name given to the invention of Albert and Abner Greenleaf and John B. Logan, who demonstrated it in 1879. Also known as

ABOVE: A truck-based, heavy-duty Sterling pumper.

OPPOSITE: An appliance with purpose-designed forward-control extended cab and body.

FIRE ENGINES

the Greenleaf Water Tower, it was mounted on trunnions and had a 1-inch (25-mm) extension pipe which ran up a main mast to 50ft (15m). It was raised by hand-cranking, the main mast braced against back pressure from a cable. FDNY bought a Greenleaf tower, despite seeing it overturn during acceptance tests, and the stability of water towers was always seen as a weak point thereafter.

In any case, only a few Greenleaf towers were actually bought, as they were soon overtaken by George C. Hale's tower of 1889, which was raised by a chemical-hydraulic system.

FEMCO (the Fire Extinguisher Maintenance Co.), which had taken over the Greenleaf patent, responded with the new Champion, still raised by hand-cranking, but the fact that it was mounted on a turntable meant it could operate at an angle out of the vertical. It was a great success.

FIRE ENGINES

What was possibly the ultimate water tower was that designed by Henry H. Gorton of the San Francisco Fire Department in 1898. This used the water pump's motor to raise the tower, which could be swung through 70 degrees and 35 degrees away from the vertical while in operation. Complete flexibility was ensured by means of a ball-and-socket joint in the supply pipe, which allowed the nozzle to rotate 360 degrees in the horizontal and nearly 180 degrees vertically. The Gorton tower was able to reach 76ft (23m), making it the highest ever for its time. It had such a huge capacity, being fed by eight 3-in (76-mm) inlets, that four steam pumpers with a total output of 4,500gpm were needed to satisfy its thirst.

By 1905, however, there were only two players in the market. Seagrave produced a spring-assisted machine while American LaFrance delivered the first motorized water tower, as opposed to one converted to tractor-pulling, in 1914. In fact, it was tractorization, just as it had been with the old steam pumps, that kept many water towers in

service when they would otherwise have been scrapped. The final towers, built from the late 1920s onwards, were mostly hydraulically-raised, though the last commercial example, delivered to Los Angeles in 1938, was spring-raised.

BIG ENGINES, BIG PUMPS

The 1920s and '30s would see further developments in firefighting technology on both sides of the Atlantic, with closed cabs providing more safety and comfort. Mid-mounted pumps were easier to use, while their pneumatic tyres and powerful diesel engines made them faster and more efficient on the road.

But the smaller, less affluent fire departments could not necessarily afford big, heavy and fast machines, and they may not have even needed them. Indeed, a 1926 conference of the National Fire Brigades Association in England concluded that smaller, lighter engines of 200–250gpm were actually more effective than the bigger ones in rural and suburban areas, with their narrower roads and the possibility of rougher terrain, and that the heavyweight 700–1000-gpm machines should be left to function in industrial, warehousing and docklands districts.

The Barton front-mounted pump was ideal for smaller brigades and departments. Bolted in front of the radiator, it took its power directly from the engine's crankshaft, and so needed no power take-off or linkage. The Barton weighed a mere 20lbs (9kg) and could be fitted by any competent mechanic, usually to a Ford Model T or later Model A, while still pumping 200–250gpm. Front-mounted pumps were less common in the UK, where they were thought to be vulnerable to damage, but some American-made Bartons were fitted to utility escape units during the Second World War.

By the mid-1920s, private cars had long since made the transition to pneumatic tyres, and from 1922 pneumatics were also fitted to small pumpers such as the Dennis 250/300-gpm turbine and the equivalent Merryweather. But conventional wisdom had it that solid tyres were still the best choice for heavyweight engines where both high-speed capability and fuel consumption were concerned. All this changed, however, when Dunlop developed heavy-duty pneumatic tyres for trucks, and promoted their use on fire engines as well. London's first pneumatic-tyred appliance was a

Dennis 500/600-gpm pump in 1928, the results of which were spectacular; the Twickenham Fire Brigade, for example, discovered that its Dennis was 4–6mph (2.5–10km/h) faster after it had abandoned solid tyres.

Six-wheeled pumps were becoming popular at around the same time, and Morris Commercial promoted its six-wheeled chassis as performing better across rough ground than a four-wheeler with a trailer pump. Merryweather produced an interesting six-wheeler for the War Office in 1929, based on a Thornycroft, and with caterpillar tracks that could be fitted to the rear four wheels in a matter of minutes when the going got sticky.

Multi-purpose fire engines were also making an appearance in the late 1920s. Ahrens-Fox of the USA, which was regarded as an industry leader in that decade, launched the Skirmisher in 1928. This was a light engine, but it was an innovation in that it was the first truly integrated quadruple machine, carrying pump, hose, booster tank and service ladder. With a rotary pump of

600 or 750gpm, it was a foreshadow of later multi-purpose machines.

Earlier in the 1920s, other manufacturers had offered pump escapes, which carried both the means of fighting a fire (the pump) and of effecting rescues (a ladder). This advent of firefighting vehicles that were able to 'multi-task' was a great step forward, eliminating the need for several different vehicles to attend a fire.

In the three decades since the heyday of the horse-drawn fire engine, technology had leapt ahead, yet in body design, the simple, open layout, with neither seating nor weather protection for the firefighters, had barely changed. But what had been acceptable on a 10-mph (16-km/h) horse-drawn engine no longer applied on a 50-mph (80-km/h) pumper, from which firefighters could be thrown off at speed while clinging precariously to the ladder or standing on the rear platform. In a reply to calls for a safer engine, Dennis introduced the New World cabs in 1928, which provided firemen with secure inward-facing seats. One of these was put to the test on Dundee Fire Brigade's Leyland pump, which had been given a New World body, but which skidded off an icy

road and into a ditch while on a call. No one was hurt, however, and within five minutes the pumper was back on the road.

Other manufacturers soon followed suit, even though the New World and similar open cabs still didn't protect firefighters from the elements. Pirsch was the first in America to fit a fully enclosed cab on a 1928 custom-built pumper, though the company never really exploited its breakthrough, and Seagrave launched a closed cab in 1937, with a canopy extending rearwards over a bench seat. There were also fully-enclosed designs, in what was known as sedan-style in America and limousine-in Britain. Some of these, especially those of the later 1930s, were elegant machines that really did evoke luxury limousines, though others, it has to be said, were more like buses.

Meanwhile, there had also been developments in ladder technology. Back in 1923, Ahrens-Fox had launched a four-wheeled, tractor-hauled aerial with Dahill Air Hoists to raise the ladders. Another innovation, often seen in city engines, was to mount the ground ladders on the sides of the vehicle, which lowered its centre of gravity and improved stability.

A few years later, however, and Ahrens was finding it difficult to weather the early 1930s, its orders plummeting in those austere times. The company, known for its expensive, custom-built machines, responded with the cheaper Junior Model V, based on a commercial chassis, but it also launched the large and expensive Tower Aerial. This had a wooden aerial ladder with a tower nozzle mounted on the end, thus combining the capabilities of both water tower and rescue ladder. It was an idea ahead of its time that didn't really come into its own until the widespread acceptance of steel ladders 20 years later.

Ladders enabled Pirsch to survive the Depression. It launched the first all-powered lifting ladder in 1930, using two hydraulic cylinders to do the work. Only one man was needed to operate the system, and better still, during those years when few departments could afford to spend out on new equipment, Pirsch offered the hydraulic system as an upgrade that could be fitted to existing ladders. Pirsch also pioneered metal ladders, delivering a 100-ft (30-m) system in 1935, and in the late '30s launched the

latticework aluminium ladder that would become its trademark innovation.

With the plethora of different apparatus now available, it was hardly surprising that the range of machines on offer should not have grown too. Take Mack as an example: in 1930 it listed the Junior range of smaller pumpers as the 500-gpm Type 45 and 600-gpm, 100-hp (74.6-kW) Type 55. Then there was the Type 50, another small engine, but which was available as a triple combination. It was followed by the medium-sized Type 70, but for real power, there was the 140-hp (104.4-kW) Type 75, with a large six-cylinder engine and four-wheel brakes, plus the choice of rotary or centrifugal 750-gpm pumps, while at the top of the range, the larger still Type 95 also had a 1000-gpm option. There were, of course, other choices, and the range swelled in the following years to include the streamlined Type 80 of 1938 and many more. Pump-power was increasing, too, the most powerful Mack pumper ever made being a 1500-gpm unit built for Wilmington, Delaware.

Pumps were also moving location, the traditional position being at the vehicle's rear, but the increasing practice of carrying an escape ladder as well meant that it had to be removed to get to the controls. The solution was to mount the pump within the wheelbase, with its controls also mid-mounted for easy access. This made pump maintenance more difficult, but allowed faster access to the controls at the scene of a fire.

Bigger pumps, larger, heavier machines carrying more and varied equipment, and a general expectation of greater performance on the road, all added up to a need for more power, to which manufacturers responded. American LaFrance's solution was an impressive V12 power unit launched in 1931. It was based on two six-cylinder engines spliced together, delivering 240hp (179kW), and would stay in production for 30 years, powering trucks and buses as well as fire engines.

LaFrance actually built some appliances with two power units in case one was not enough. They were made specifically for the city of Los Angeles in 1938, and were named Metropolitan Duplexes, in that they consisted of two 240-hp V12s powering a pair of two-stage 1000-gpm pumps. The Duplex came with a manifold wagon that travelled with it, whose job it was to handle the distribution of this powerful system that supplied up to 20 outlets. Two later Duplexes offered a 3000-gpm capacity, the idea being that such massive rigs would reduce the number of fire engines needed, and thus reduce confusion and congestion at a major fire. A Duplex, it was claimed, was able to do the work of three conventional pumpers.

Engine developments were not only centred on power, but it was also essential for fire engines to be able to start immediately when called, and some were fitted with two or even three ignition systems to ensure reliability. To keep engines warm and ready for use, some full-time brigades started the motor every four hours, letting it run for a few minutes. Other innovations of the 1930s were electric engine heaters and battery chargers.

Diesel engines finally began to make inroads in the late 1930s, when Leyland Motors introduced its 8.6-litre unit for fire engines in 1937. It offered 100hp (74.6kW), yet fuel consumption was 35 per cent lower than it had been in a comparable petrol unit. Nor were diesels lacking in performance, and the London Fire Brigade ran a Leyland FT3A limousine that accelerated to 40mph (64km/h) in 31 seconds, and which was able to deliver 830gpm at 100psi. New Stutz launched a 1000-gpm diesel pumper in 1939 in the USA, powered by Cummins, which failed to benefit the company greatly, for it went out of business the following year. Even so, diesel power was finally here to stay.

LOOKING FORWARD

The two decades following the Second World War saw many advances in fire engine technology: cab-forward designs, closed and tilting cabs; the universal acceptance of diesel engines; better radio communications; metal aerials, and the first snorkels. The war had seen a suspension of development as manufacturers concentrated on military work, but the money was unavailable for new equipment in any case, and many fire departments and brigades were forced to struggle on using pre-war equipment.

In Britain, in anticipation of air raids on major cities, the government had ordered the production of cheaper mass-produced pumpers from 1937. The pumps were driven by secondary engines, rather than power takeoffs, and were less sophisticated than peacetime appliances. Yet these 'utility' machines gave good accounts of themselves, there being two basic versions. The heavy unit was based on a medium truck chassis from Austin, Morris, Ford or Bedford, with a 700-gpm two-stage pump, either a Leyland-engined Gwynne or a Ford-engined Sulzer. The extra-heavy unit used a Gwynne single-stage 1100-gpm pump, with 7-in (178-mm) suction and six outlets on an Austin or Bedford chassis. Alongside these were water tankers, known as dam lorries, which were flat platform trucks with 500-gallon water tanks on board. Tanks were made either of steel-framed canvas or of galvanized iron, and the dam lorries were used wherever the water supply was likely to be restricted. They were termed mobile dams when towing a trailer pump.

After the war, lack of resources in what came to be known as austerity Britain meant that many of these wartime utility appliances had to keep going, even though they had a lower life expectancy than the sturdier pre-war engines, which could be expected to serve for 15 years. A 1949 report by HM Chief Inspector of Fire Services found that of the 1,667 pumpers in England and Wales, nearly half were

Volvo chassis are also popular in the UK.

still wartime utilities, and over 300 were more than 15 years old, with only 12 new pumpers having been delivered since the end of the war. But from 1949, fire authorities were finally able to order new machines, and over the next few years, Britain's fire fleet was gradually renewed.

Just about all of these were cab-forward, also known as forward-control appliances, and represented a revolution that had begun tentatively in Britain before the war. In the USA, American LaFrance had introduced its own cab-forward design in 1944, though it too had been restricted by wartime work, and the new Series 700 did not go on sale for another three years. Placing the cab in front of the engine had many advantages, in that the visibility of the driver was greatly improved, and with a shorter wheelbase the whole rig was more manoeuvrable and tighter-turning. It also allowed a more efficient use of space, freeing up the rear of the appliance for carrying equipment. Engine access was somewhat trickier, however, though the problem was later solved by the tilting

LEFT: Saxon built this appliance on a Volvo chassis.

ABOVE: A graphic message to the public warning of the dangers of fire.

cab. White offered the first tilt-cab chassis as early as 1949, and Mack followed nine years later.

Not all American manufacturers followed the cab-forward LaFrance at

FIRE ENGINES

OPPOSITE: Overhead ladders are now accessible from ground level.

BELOW: Note the trio of spotlights on the roof.

once; Mack didn't offer such an appliance until 1956, and that only came via its purchase of C.D. Beck, owner of Ahrens-Fox. The ex-Ahrens design went on to become Mack's successful C-85 and C-95 cab-forward engines, with 750-gpm and 1000-gpm pumps respectively. Both were powered

by the company's own six-cylinder Thermodyne engine, with its optional automatic transmission.

But LaFrance's cab-forward Series 700 didn't necessarily include a closed cab, which was still an option. In fact, it remained the norm for US-built fire engines to be left open to the elements. There were exceptions, of course: Seagrave had offered its fully enclosed Safety Sedan from as early as 1936, though the only major customer for it had been the Detroit Fire Department, and although Seagrave kept the Sedan

in production right up to 1960, only a few were sold to other departments. It wasn't until the mid-1960s that closed cabs became widespread on US fire engines, and the main motivation even then appears to have been the increasing incidence of riots and civil disturbances, and the fact that closed cabs afforded firefighters protection from flying bricks and bottles.

By contrast, just about all British fire engines of the post-war era came with fully enclosed cabs, including those coming from Dennis,

Merryweather and the group of smaller companies that sprang into being after the Second World War. Open appliances could still be made to order, and what is believed to be the last such built in Britain was delivered by Dennis to the glass-maker Pilkington in 1956.

Alongside the advent of safer, weatherproof cabs came advances in aerial design. Wood, used in heavy ladders, was being replaced by steel or a lighter alloy, and in 1949 Merryweather was exporting 50-ft (15-m) three-section alloy ladders to

FIRE ENGINES

OPPOSITE: A well-equipped pumper belonging to Maine's Kennebunk Fire-Rescue Service.

RIGHT: Even smaller pumpers come fully-equipped.

BELOW: A German MAN-based pumper.

Australia, which were soon adopted by the home market as well. Kent Fire Brigade was the first, intending to replace its entire fleet of bulky, heavyweight wheeled escapes. There were good arguments for doing so, in that the alloy units weighed 250lbs (113kg), which was only one-seventh

that of the old wooden escapes, and at £200 cost less than one-third of the price. An additional benefit was that alloy ladders took up far less space, often allowing more appliances to squeeze into fire stations. Not that all British wheeled escapes disappeared at once, however, for the final one wasn't pensioned off until 1994.

Another significant development, as far as escapes were concerned, was the famous articulated boom with a secure platform on top for one or two men which was to eliminate the ladder altogether. In the late 1950s, Chicago's Fire Commissioner, Robert J. Quinn, had been looking for something to replace the department's three antiquated water towers, which were in any case no longer available. He had been watching tree-trimmers in the city

FIRE ENGINES

Massive units based on commercial truck chassis are a US speciality.

using trucks with hydraulically-operated elevating arms that lifted them in baskets high into the air, and which allowed the men to move up and down or from side to side at will, rotating through 360 degrees. Quinn saw how something similar could offer firefighters a way of manoeuvring themselves into position over a fire. He decided to take the quicker and cheaper route of giving the job to the department's own maintenance shop, rather than to a manufacturer, which obtained a standard 50-ft articulated boom and basket from Pitman Manufacturing and mounted it on a standard truck chassis. A length of hose was attached along the boom, connected to a 2-in (51-mm) nozzle in the basket. The result was the first elevating platform in the industry, and it was quickly dubbed Quinn's Snorkel because of its amazing ability to reach inside blazing buildings; it worked so well that the Snorkel Fire Equipment Company was set up, based in St. Joseph, Missouri, to make even more, and telescopic booms were soon added to the standard

articulating types, which were easier to use in constricted spaces.

Throughout the 1950s Mack and American LaFrance were the undoubted market leaders in the USA. They had seen rivals such as Buffalo and Ahrens-Fox fall by the wayside, but there was still room for smaller companies to survive or even make new forays into the market. Howe, for example, offered an innovative pump control panel up behind the cab, giving the operator a much better view, while Pirsch was well-respected for its aerial and combination appliances. Ward LaFrance (no connection with the market leader) was a favourite of FDNY, while Crown Body & Coach was a bus-builder that diversified into fire engines in 1949. It was a similar story in the UK, where the market was dominated by Dennis and Merryweather, but where several smaller concerns were also thriving; Hampshire Car Bodies, Wilsdon & Co. and Carmichael were only a few profiting from the need to renew Britain's post-war fire fleet, which by 1955, according to the chairman of Dennis, was finally achieved.

Multi-purpose appliances were becoming more popular, and in 1951

the Essex Fire Brigade in England ordered four machines that could operate as either pump escapes or water tenders, as the need arose. Based on Dodge 125 chassis, and equipped with Dennis mid-mounted pumps, they had two water tanks of 100 and 300 gallons respectively. The appliance used the smaller tank only as a pump escape, the demountable pump being removed to allow the fitting of a 50-ft wheeled escape. As a water tender, with only an extension ladder, both tanks were kept filled.

Some of Britain's most famous fire engines appeared in the mid-1950s. These were the romantically-named 'Green Goddesses', a large fleet of which was maintained nationally to support local brigades in emergencies, which in 1955 was presumed to be nuclear war. Despite the dark-green colour, the Green Goddesses were not under direct military control, but were wheeled out of storage as the need arose. They gained particular fame during a national firemen's strike in the late 1970s, and made their final call-outs in 2002, by which time they were nearly 50 years old. They were sold off as collectors' items soon afterwards.

FIRE ENGINES

This appliance has a standard cab but plenty of room for equipment.

There were incremental improvements in the 1960s, rather than major steps forward. In 1964 the English Kent Fire Brigade asked its members to come up with ideas, and some of these were incorporated into a Commer VAKS-based fire engine built by HCB-Angus. It was an adaptable machine, able to run as a water tender, water tender ladder, pump, pump ladder, or pump salvage tender. The equipment was positioned for easy access at exactly the right height, an example being the slide-out BA rack.

Americans, it is said, like things big, and that was certainly true of the aptly named Super Pumper. Built by Mack, and delivered to FDNY in 1965, this was quite simply the most powerful land-based fire appliance ever made. It echoed the thinking behind Los Angeles's Metropolitan Pumper of 1938, the idea being that one giant rig would do the work of several smaller ones, reducing congestion at the fire scene. The difference was that while the Metropolitan had been designed to do the work of three appliances, the Super Pumper was able to do that of ten.

It was a monster, designed for major fires that might occur in New York's high-rise district. Carried on a semi-trailer, the massive pump was based around a Napier-Deltic diesel engine, normally used for powering railroad locomotives or small naval vessels, and was rated at 2400hp (1789.7kW) at 1800rpm. The engine alone weighed 14,000lbs (6350kg), but it was needed to power the DeLaval Turbine six-stage centrifugal pump, which could draw from as many as eight hydrants and deliver an astonishing 10,000gpm at 300psi. The entire thing was mounted on a semi-trailer, hauled by a Mack six-wheeled F-Series diesel tractor.

In places where eight hydrants were not available, the Super Pumper's sister appliance, the Super Tender, was used, which was equipped with an 8-in (203-mm) Stang monitor and 2,000ft (610m) of 4-in (102-mm) hose. This, in turn, was supplemented by three C-Series Satellite Tenders, each with 6-in (152-mm) 4000-gpm Stang monitors.

The Super Pumper, and its various attendants, may have seemed like the sort of machine built to attract publicity, rather than fight fires, but it really did see service, making over 2,000

FIRE ENGINES

This FFA Intruder has a custom-built chassis.

runs before it was finally retired in 1982, in the event of which a fleet of six double-unit 2000-gpm pumpers was needed to replace it.

EFFICIENCY & STANDARDIZATION

The Super Pumper may have been one of a kind, which didn't mean that conventional fire engines had been starved of power. By the mid-1960s diesel had become the fuel of choice, even though some of the smaller American pumpers retained their petrol power. But diesel's overall efficiency was particularly attractive, graphically demonstrated in a Mack C-95 in 1964 when the 1000-gpm pumper worked continuously for seven days, delivering over ten million gallons of water at a cost of 1,100 gallons of diesel. Soon afterwards, most Mack fire engines were diesel-powered, and FDNY was soon running an all-diesel fleet.

The most effective means of improving a diesel engine's power and torque is to turbocharge it, and from the late 1960s fire engines followed trucks in using turbo-diesel engines.

Ford was a leading proponent, offering a turbo in its D600 truck range, which HCB-Angus built into fire engines, while Merryweather's Marksman range could also be based on the Ford turbo-diesel truck chassis. A more radical solution had been attempted back in 1960, but while the turbo-diesel would become an industry standard, the alternative turned out to be a dead end. This was the gas turbine fitted to an American LaFrance Series-900 chassis. The turbine was a 325-hp (242.3-kW) from Boeing, and a few were built into appliances, with San Francisco buying a 1000-gpm triple combination pumper, and Seattle ordering a turbine-powered 100-ft (30-m) tractor-hauled aerial. It all looked good on paper, but in practice the turbine 900s were slow to accelerate and hard to brake, with none of the instant response needed in heavy traffic, and they were noisy into the bargain. The experiment was swiftly abandoned, and all the turbine 900s were converted to petrol power.

Gas turbines may have come to nought, but compressed-air tools were becoming increasingly useful, in that fire engines were more frequently being called to rescue crash victims trapped inside vehicles. In 1966, Dennis

77

exhibited a dual-purpose machine which featured a built-in compressor to supply air tools via one of its Dean 180-ft (55-m) hose reels, thus enabling it to deliver jets of water and operate compressed-air tools at the same time.

These developments were all concerned with the performance of fire engines on the road and at the scene of a fire, but there was still room for improvement where the safety of firefighters was concerned. A 1972 study by the Institution of Fire Engineers found that 10 per cent of fire-service accidents occurred in or on appliances, and half of these involved getting in or out of vehicles. This brought into sharp relief the compromises involved in using commercial truck chassis. They may have been cheaper than custom chassis, with easy maintenance and a good spares backup, but there were inevitable shortcomings in that they had not been designed with a specific use in mind.

In response, Loughborough Consultants designed an appliance, the Chubb Pacesetter, based on a Reynolds Boughton chassis. Unveiled at Interfire's equipment show in 1975, it had a lower stance than a conventional fire engine, and the six-man cab offered

a low-level entrance and a door that was 4-ft (1.2-m) wide for quick and easy entry/exit. There was low-level ladder access, and the suction hose was also mounted lower down, in lockers between the wheels. Unusually, the Pacesetter was rear-engined, its General Motors 236-hp (176-kW) V6 diesel driving through an Allison automatic transmission. In the event, only two of these innovative machines were sold in the UK, but they undoubtedly contributed to forward thinking within the industry.

There were other attempts to inject some fresh ideas into the industry in the mid-1980s. Timoney, of County Meath in Ireland, developed an appliance with independent suspension based on that of an armoured personnel carrier. It bore a resemblance to the Chubb Pacesetter of a decade earlier, and was slightly more successful in that 19 were built, it being too expensive to sell in large numbers. In 1987, Reynolds Boughton unveiled another fire engine resembling the Pacesetter: the Brigadier water tender boasted a safety cab and a low centre of gravity, and was the result of a two-year consultation exercise with brigades. But as with its predecessors,

There is a big front platform on this latest-specification rig.

these good ideas failed to be translated into firm orders.

Even if brigades and departments could not always afford innovative new appliances, legislation was able to force improvements. From 1990, the European Committee for Standardization began to consider setting common standards for new appliances across Europe. The idea was to ease trade between EC members, rather than formulate a standard design of fire engine. Thus the Manual Handling Regulations from 1993 influenced equipment stowage, introducing slide-out trays and slide-and-tilt drawers as well as swing-out panels. Working on the roof of an engine was effectively outlawed, which meant that ladders had to be accessed from ground level. Whatever the motivation for these regulations, they often ended up making life that much easier for the firefighter.

More attention was also paid to security in the 1990s, echoing the American move towards closed cabs 30 years earlier. Sadly, fire crews were increasingly coming under physical attack, and features such as central locking, and mesh screens over windows, sought to protect them more effectively. There were advances in materials as the 1990s progressed, seen in the Dennis Rapier, with its Metawall body panels. These were formed from a composite material strong enough to replace the traditional plywood, but still light enough to be built onto Dennis's tubular stainless-steel spaceframe chassis. There would be many more advances into the 21st century, many of them concerned with the safety of fire engines as much as with their performance. Meanwhile, the appliances themselves were becoming ever more specialized and high-tech, demonstrating the many advances made since the days of the first steam pumpers.

MERRYWEATHER:
AN OLD AND TRUSTED NAME

*A*lthough it went out of business over 30 years ago, for more than a century Merryweather was one of the best-known names in the fire engine business, its origins stretching back further than any of its contemporaries to 1750, when Adam Nuttall began building manual fire pumps in London. By 1792 the company was a partnership, named Hadley, Simpkins and Lott, and had introduced some of the first successful horse-drawn pumps. It was in 1807 that Moses Merryweather arrived as an apprentice, and by 1839 he was in complete control and the company bore his name.

Merryweather was a pioneer not only of steam pumps but also of horse-drawn manuals, building its first in 1861 for a private brigade. Named Deluge, it lived up to its name by being highly effective, and was soon followed by the more powerful two-cylinder Torrent. In 1863, Merryweather won first prize at the Crystal Palace National Steam Engine Contest, and from then on its prosperity was assured.

The company's first self-propelled steam fire engine was unveiled in 1899, the evocatively named Fire King delivering a water jet 150-ft (46-m) high at 350gpm. Just as impressively, it was also able to maintain 20mph (32km/h) on a flat road, long after the strongest team of horses would have grown tired, with the result that Fire Kings were soon being substituted for horse-drawn steamers all over Britain.

Within a few years, Merryweather had introduced another innovation, this being the world's first fire engine with a petrol engine powering both the pump and the appliance itself. The first of these went to Baron de Rothschild's estate in France in 1904, and the second to the Finchley Fire Brigade in north London later in the same year. Both machines were powered by four-cylinder 30-hp (22.4-kW) engines, with a 250-gpm Hatfield pump, a 60-gallon soda-acid chemical engine, a 180-ft (55-m) hose-reel and a wheeled escape. Merryweather also experimented with battery-electric power, but the rapid improvement of petrol engines soon rendered the concept obsolete.

Merryweather had long been associated with turntable ladders, and it produced its first as early as 1908, which used engine power to both rotate and extend the 65-ft (20-m) ladder. By the 1930s, the company was building steel ladders mounted on turntables, as well as its highly respected reciprocating pumps. It also pioneered the use of foam systems.

The company launched its long-running Marquis series in 1954, based on an AEC-Maudesley chassis, even though truck-maker AEC would supply many of the post-war Merryweather chassis. The first Marquis was designed as a light appliance for both urban and rural brigades, available as both water tender and pump. The Derbyshire Fire Service commissioned an emergency tender version in 1957, based on an AEC diesel, the equipment including a 12,000-lb (5445-kg) winch, driven from a power take-off, a 10-hp (7.5-kW) generator, and an Epco hydraulic lifting set.

Meanwhile, Merryweather was not neglecting its famous turntables, having built an example that was hydraulically powered as early as 1924. But in the late 1950s hydraulics finally replaced engine power for good. The first of these was an AEC-based appliance with a 100-ft (30-m) ladder, and others soon followed. By 1966, the Marquis had reached Series 7, with power steering and rear-facing crew seats. A 625-gpm pump was standard, fitted either in the rear or midships, and there was an entire range of different tank and ladder options. Merryweather delivered its last turntables in the early 1970s before finally closing down.

CHAPTER TWO
PUMPERS: WORKHORSES
OF THE FLEET

Whatever specialized appliances may be called for – water tenders, aerials or rescue tenders – a pumper will inevitably also be on the scene. In the USA, pumpers outnumber ladder trucks by three or four to one, so they are also the most common

appliances of all, which doesn't mean they are all the same. What follows is a description of the various options and equipment that can be fitted to the modern US-built pumper. Although the pumper is often the basis of a combination appliance that can do

BELOW: A fine shot of a pumper with mid-mounted controls.

OPPOSITE: A basic pumper, its equipment stowed neatly inside.

several different jobs, carrying not only ladders and foam equipment, for

example, but also water-pumping gear, the design can also be specified to suit individual departments. In fact, many of the features mentioned below apply equally to other specialized appliances besides pumpers.

CHASSIS/POWER UNITS
The first and most basic distinction in pumper design is the chassis. For decades, all fire engines were based on commercial truck chassis, which made sense from many points of view, these often being mass-produced and therefore far cheaper than the custom-builts. Some municipal authorities may use the same commercial chassis right across their fleets, and if the fire departments use them too, spares sourcing, maintenance and training of mechanics becomes far simpler and easier to effect. Commercial chassis, moreover, are also proven designs with a good record of reliability, and while the design may be standard, departments can choose, depending on what the appliance-maker offers, from any of the

major truck-makers, such as Ford, General Motors, Freightliner, IHC, Peterbilt, Kenworth and others. With the chassis supplied, the job of the appliance-maker is to design and build the body.

But another option emerged from the 1990s, that of the custom-built chassis. For all its advantages, the commercial chassis is always a compromise, never having been designed with fire department use in

mind, so may need to be modified to make it suitable for the task. Take the suspension, for example: standard truck suspension is designed to carry heavy loads at relatively low speeds, so it has to be tough and low-cost. But

FIRE ENGINES

A massive windshield maximizes visibility.

fire engines need to get to places quickly, which reveals the limitations of basic truck suspension, especially when cornering, which is why increasing numbers of appliance manufacturers are now fitting different suspension systems.

Some have chosen proprietary air systems, while Pierce has actually designed its own torsion bar independent system, the TAK-4. Ferrara, too, has taken this route, but has used a coil-sprung system, claimed to be more compact than torsion bars. Pierce claims many advantages for TAK-4 over a standard live-axle truck system. First, it reduces stopping distances, due to having 17-in (432-mm) vented disc brakes in place of the standard 15-inch and, according to Pierce, needs 23 per cent less space in which to stop.

Ride quality is another area of improvement, and there is a more scientific means of measuring this than asking firefighters whether they feel cosseted or not. According to acclerometer tests, measuring G-force inside the cab, a leaf-sprung front end delivers 0.51g, but the TAK-4 only 0.15g, which makes it about equivalent to a Chevrolet Tahoe SUV.

It's a similar story when it comes to handling, where independent suspension, whether by torsion or coil springs, gives more stability at high speeds, as well as a tighter turning angle for greater manoeuvrability at low speeds. Finally, maintenance can be less demanding on a modern independent system than on a traditional leaf-sprung set-up, with no U-bolts to keep tight, lubricated-for-life ball joints, and no need to adjust the caster angle. And the bigger 17-in brake rotors, fitted to both Pierce and Ferrara systems, deliver longer brake life, with Pierce claiming a 56,000-mile (90120-km) pad life on one of its chassis.

Cab design is another advantage of custom-built chassis, its format being crucial to the effective performance of any fire truck. It has to be large enough to accommodate five or six fire crew in safety and comfort, with four big doors to allow them quick and easy entry and exit, while a raised-roof section at the rear may be needed for the pump control panel. Some fire departments favour a particular seating arrangement, or may need room for the specialized tools they are often called upon to use, while rearwards of the cab, the appliance body must be able to stow a wide variety of equipment.

In the end, it all comes down to what the individual department needs, and how much it can afford to spend. The pattern is that medium-sized and large pumpers are increasingly using custom-built chassis, although commercial chassis are still the norm where small pumpers are concerned.

The market for pumpers is relatively small, even in the USA, and can never justify the building of engines and transmissions specifically for them. Fortunately, the wide range of heavy truck components are just as suitable, and builders currently have the choice of only a few specialists. Axles are usually supplied by Rockwell, Eaton and Meritor, while Fuller and Spicer build manual transmissions, though Eaton Fuller now produces an automatic in the CEEMAT. In fact, automatic transmissions are becoming increasingly popular, in that they are far more efficient and responsive and also eliminate the need for clutch replacement. Allison, with its heavy

truck autos, completely dominates the market in these, with a choice of four-, five- or six-speed transmissions.

When it comes to power units, diesel now reigns supreme, apart from in some mini-pumpers, thanks to its greater fuel economy, whether built by Detroit Diesel, Caterpillar or Cummins. The famous Detroit Diesel two-strokes, specifically the 6V and 8V, used to be the favourites of many appliance-makers but, unable to meet current emissions legislation, have been superseded by the new generation of four-stroke Detroits, which use less fuel as well as pumping out fewer emissions. The Series 40, 50 and 60 offer a wide range of outputs from 155 to 500hp (115.6–372.8kW).

All of these have electronic injection controls, which maximize both power and economy; but the electronics are there not merely to improve engine performance. Detroit Diesel's Electronic Fire Commander is designed specifically for the fire appliance market, combining a pressure sensor governor controller with a monitor of the engine and

A Mercedes-based six-wheeler with roof-mounted nozzle.

pump system while the pump is in operation. Temperature, oil pressure and engine speed are also monitored, keeping the operator fully informed and allowing him to change engine speed as the pump requires.

But although electronic engine control has great benefits, it also complicates the build process. Non-electronic diesels, as long as they could be physically bolted in, could be fitted in any chassis, but engine electronics need to be integrated with those of the whole vehicle, which includes the pump, which is the reason why some makers specify only one engine to save costs. As well as Detroit Diesel, Cummins engines are also popular, specifically the ISB, ISC, IM and M11+ units of 175 to 500hp, the ISB and ISC being fully electronic up to 350hp (261kW), while the 500-hp ISM is available only to the fire service, reflecting the importance of that particular market. Caterpillar has long been a market leader in diesel, and its fire engine power units of choice are the CFE, C-10 and C-12, offering 175 to 455hp (130.5–339.3kW).

Gone are the days when all fire engines had their engines in the front. Cab-forward designs have not only

hidden the engine away, but have also widened the possibility of where it is mounted. It can be front, mid- or rear-mounted, the latter producing the quietest ride for the crew and liberating more cab space. Choosing the basics of a pumper, therefore – the chassis, engine and transmission –

opens up a whole range of options, though for many departments there may be a different bottom line. A fully-equipped custom chassis can come with a price tag of over $200,000, while a commercial chassis with more basic features may cost only half that sum, presenting a persuasive

argument for even the most discerning of fire chiefs.

ABOVE: This may be Mercedes-based, but it has not been custom-made.

OPPOSITE: The secret of the modern pumper is to be able to pack a huge amount of equipment into a tight space.

FIRE ENGINES

CABS/BODIES

Just as the options for chassis, engines and all running gear have multiplied, so too have those for cabs. In the old days, firefighters clung onto tailboards as their appliances raced to emergencies, and injuries were therefore common, with men being flung off at speed. Then small jump seats were fitted, though often without seat belts or any protection from the weather. Now, regulations insist that all firefighters are

PUMPERS: WORKHORSES OF THE FLEET

Safety guidelines not only insist on enclosed cabs but also have to meet quietness standards (gone are the days when it was thought acceptable to deafen firefighters with the noise of engine and siren) and be highly visible, with reflective stripes to make them obvious to motorists. Many fire departments now equip their crews with headsets as well, providing the double benefit of protecting their hearing and permitting them to communicate, allowing them to decide how best to tackle the emergency once they arrive. A communication headset is especially useful for the pump operator once on scene, for being isolated from the other crew, and perhaps unable to see what is going on, it will enable him/her to be kept up to date.

The main pumper body presents yet other choices, firstly the material from which it is to be made. Traditionally, pumper bodies have been fabricated from sheets of galvanneal steel, welded together, but aluminium is becoming increasingly popular for its

carried inside fully-enclosed cabs, and that factory-installed belts are worn.

Commercial cabs, with seating for only two or three people, and two doors, aren't really suitable for this purpose unless modified. Purpose-designed fire cabs have seating for up to six, with four doors, sometimes built tall enough to allow firefighters to stand while wearing helmets. The position of the second pair of doors is another variable, being sometimes rear-facing, when the cab is referred to as a short four-door (SFD). A medium four-door (MFD) has all four doors on the sides, with the rear pair straddling the front wheels, while a long four-door (LFD) extends the cab, with the rear pair behind the front wheels.

lightness (thus allowing more equipment to be carried) and resistance to corrosion. Aluminium bodies are made from a combination of extrusions, known for their strength, and flat panels. Custom Fire makes a selling point of the fact that its bodies are bolted rather than welded together. Modular construction is another recent innovation, allowing different sections of the body to be built up separately before being finally assembled on the chassis. This makes the build process easier, not to mention repair work.

From the outside, pumper bodies often resemble big boxes, but the way in which they are divided up to carry equipment and water is an art in itself. Thirty years ago, things were much simpler, with most bodies featuring two low-mounted compartments on each side, with ground ladders mounted above them on the passenger side, and possibly hard suction hoses on the other. In the late 1970s to early '80s, there was an increasing trend towards high-sided compartments as well, that ran from the pump panel to the rear. These more than doubled the storage space available, which was particularly useful as fire crews began to use breathing apparatus on a regular basis.

These high-sided compartments are still standard features in many pumpers, but even here there are choices to be made. Take the doors, for instance: the standard door hinges outward, like the cab door, but these can get in the way when crew are moving around the appliance at a fire scene. Upward opening doors get around this problem, and are becoming increasingly popular, having the side benefit of protecting crew beneath them from the rain. The European tradition is to use roll-up shutter-style doors, and these are finding favour with US manufacturers as well. They have a distinct advantage in that if a door were to pop open as the appliance is being driven out of quarters, it may be sheared off as it hits the side of the building, which doesn't happen in the case of shutter doors.

Ladder storage has changed over the years, the current practice being overhead mounting, accessible from the rear, thus placing the ladders out of the way but easy to access. Sometimes they are mid-mounted over the hosebed and through a special compartment that runs through the water tank. Hose, even more than the ladder, is fundamental to a pumper's purpose, and the industry body, the National Fire Protection Association (NFPA) specifies a minimum of 400ft (120m) of attack hose, used for delivering water onto the fire, and 1,200ft (365m) of supply line from a water source for Class A pumpers. This is only a minimum, and pumpers will often carry

Water is still the favoured option for fighting domestic fires.

several hose types and sizes, which can be colour-coded to avoid confusion. This extends to the pump control panel, where each preconnected line corresponds with the colour-coded gauges and switches. There has also been another big advance in hose design; remember when every fire station had a tall, empty tower? This was for drying out the hoses, which would become affected by mildew if they weren't thoroughly dried after every use. Modern hoses can be happily stowed when wet, which saves the fire crew work and time and means that the appliance is always ready for its next call.

PUMPS & LIGHTING

The actual water pump, the heart of every pumper, is now usually mid-mounted, although some appliances still used rear- or front-mounted pumps. Large pumpers come with pumps of 750 to 2000gpm, though mini-pumpers can be much smaller, i.e., from 250gpm upwards. The pump itself is invariably hidden behind body panels, but its control panel, which is a

FIRE ENGINES

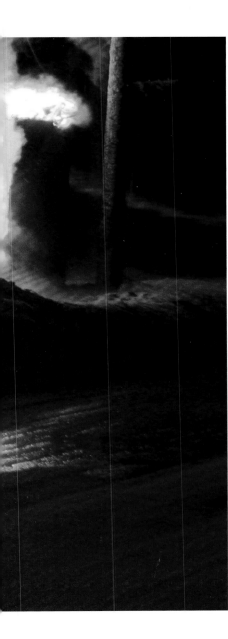

forest of dials, switches and levers, is highly visible.

Again, this can be placed just about anywhere. Side-mounting is popular, near to the pump itself, but has the disadvantage that the pump operator, sometimes referred to as the engineer, may not be able to see what is going on when standing out in a busy street. Building the panel on top of the engine, usually behind the cab, gets around this problem, and provides far better visibility, and can actually be made part of an extended cab, complete with heating or air conditioning. Of course, a top-mounted panel, especially in an extended cab, means less space is available for other equipment, illustrating the fact that pumper design will always be something of a compromise between conflicting demands.

The job of the operator at the panel is to monitor and adjust the water output to the attack hose, as well as keep an eye on the water supply. The level in the tank is indicated by means of a long vertical glass tube, though pumpers increasingly use a coloured light system, that measures the tank level in quarters. If large enough, and using different colours, these allow the

Directing the hose often needs two firefighters.

tank level to be monitored by firefighters some way from the panel, which is especially useful if the crew isn't large enough to have a pump operator permanently at the controls.

To the untrained eye, a pump panel controlling several outlets looks impossibly complex, and of course pump operators have the skill and experience to interpret them. But Saulsbury offers what it calls a diagrammatic panel, that instead of simply placing the switches and dials in rows (with or without colour coding) has a diagram of the pumper clearly showing which switch/dial relates to which outlet on the machine.

Gauges have also seen improvements. As late as 1990, gauges tended to fog up when making the transition from warm fire station to cold winter air, and once on site, the needles would flicker by 20–30lbs sq in, making it difficult to get a true reading. Filling the gauge with a liquid combination of glycerin and silicone cures both problems, preventing fogging and suppressing the action of the needle. Digital

electronic read-outs are sometimes used in place of analogue gauges, again allowing the operator to adjust the output more accurately, while electronic touch-sensitive switches are yet another advance.

But the operator may also be responsible for lighting. Pumpers can either have powerful floodlights mounted on the side, or roof-mounted light towers that can be positioned via remote control. Powered by an on-

FIRE ENGINES

are another feature of such incidents, and space has to be made for them, along with the many other tools and supplies that an adaptable pumper needs. In a well-designed pumper, every inch of space is used, with slide-out shelving providing quick and easy access.

Now take a look at a typical modern pumper, in this case one from Pierce. The pump itself, from Waterous, Hale or Darley, is mid-mounted, with 500 to 2000gpm available, and with a further option of a smaller power take-off pump of 250–1000gpm. Stainless steel pipe is used, and there is a choice of many different lighting set-ups, with portable, stationary or hydraulic generators. The pumper's body is of galvanneal steel, stainless and high-strength aluminium, with a structural warranty of ten years. There are six different body lengths from which to choose, and over 300 different body configurations, and if that were not enough, then customization is a further option.

A pumper this size is not always necessary, however. Some fire departments may need a smaller vehicle, a mini-pumper, where space is tight, where some serious all-terrain ability is needed, or simply to use as a first-response vehicle that can get to the scene before the main pumper.

A typical mini-pumper is based on a pickup truck, the Ford F550 Super Duty being a good example, with the choice of two- or four-door cab, two- or four-wheel-drive, and a five- or six-speed manual transmission. Power comes from a 6.4-litre diesel V8 of 350hp (261kW), illustrating that mini-pumpers often have as much power as their bigger brothers. An alternative base would be GMC's 4500/5500 pickup, again with the two/four-wheel drive and choice of cab doors, but with a five-speed automatic transmission and a 300-hp (223.7-kW) 6.6-litre V8 diesel. The pump itself can be 250–500gpm, driving from a power take-off, or up to 750gpm when mid-mounted, which compromises interior space but allows for a bigger pump. Pierce's mini-pump offers up to 118 cu ft (3.34m³) of storage space and a polypropylene water tank of up to 400 gallons. The tank has a lifetime warranty, and can be coupled with a 50-gallon foam tank. Options include a

board generator, such lighting is essential for night-time call-outs, especially to road crashes away from street lighting. Hydraulic rescue tools

FIRE ENGINES

60-in (5-ft) wide body, air conditioning, lighting packages, winches and foam systems.

FUTURE PUMPERS

Pumpers have seen great changes over the years, though these have recently been incremental rather than revolutionary. So what of the future? There's nothing new about non-metal bodies, and Dutch manufacturer Plastisol has been building bodies from fibreglass-reinforced polyester for some years, which have allowed water tanks to be moulded integrally with bodies, and are lighter than metal.

In 1997, E-One took this concept a stage further with the Concept 2000 prototype. Designed in partnership with General Electric, Spartech and Thermoform Plastics, Concept 2000 was aerodynamically-shaped and made from a composite polymer material. Unlike many such concepts in the vehicle industry, it actually reached production as the Daytona Series in 1999. The major mechanical components were familiar to many fire departments, i.e., Cummins engine and Allison automatic transmission, but the

The Ferrara Inundator, an industrial pumper.

polymer body made the entire vehicle a massive 20 per cent lighter than a conventional pumper. The Daytona featured midship or rear-mounted pumps of up to 1500gpm and an

aluminium-shelled cab that could seat up to eight crew.

E-One's polymer-bodied Daytona may have made it to production, but the Pierce FRV was far more of a

ABOVE: An articulated Pierce equipped with a 100-ft (30-m) ladder.

OPPOSITE: A firefighting scene in Sheffield, England.

concept than a production-ready prototype. It was a one-eighth scale model, designed to attract feedback from fire departments. FRV (First Response Vehicle) was envisaged as an ultra-adaptable vehicle combining the roles of both pumper and ambulance. It was part of a long-term trend that saw fire departments increasingly attending road crashes and other emergencies besides actual fires, the idea being that a single vehicle, combining both roles, would save sending both ambulance and fire engine to the scene of an incident.

FIRE ENGINES

The FRV would have a relatively short wheelbase, perhaps as little as 140in (3.5m), but with a four-door cab and a full-service ambulance body as well as external rescue equipment compartments, also a 300-gallon water tank, pump and hoses. It could be configured in five basic options: as an ambulance, a conventional pumper or combining the two, plus rescue and command centre options. This was modular construction taken to its logical conclusion, where the basic vehicle could be adapted to very different jobs. In firefighting, as in the animal kingdom, adaptability may well be the key to survival.

CHAPTER THREE

AERIALS: SNORKEL BOB & FRIENDS

As described in Chapter Two, aerial appliances developed from free-standing, single-length wooden ladders into extendables that were first laboriously raised by hand, using winding handles, then with assister springs, and finally by means of hydraulics. Turntable ladders had a more secure base and could be easily turned in the direction they were needed, while the ladders themselves made the transition from wood to cheaper, stronger steel, with aluminium appearing more recently as lighter

BELOW: A German aerial, showing the compact size to which a modern ladder can be reduced for stowage.

OPPOSITE: Aerials at work in Los Angeles.

alternatives. In America, the snorkel made use of existing technology, such

as the ubiquitous cherry picker, to create an hydraulic platform that could be used both to fight fires and effect rescues. The hydraulic platform, however, has not replaced the ladder, contrary to the predictions of some, but has merely provided an alternative that does a similar job. A ladder is still lighter in weight than an hydraulic platform, which allowed the appliance to carry more equipment of other types, and early platforms were, in any case, unable to match the ultimate height of ladders.

Despite all the developments in aerial devices over the decades, their two-fold job hasn't changed, which is to fight the fire from a height, often more accurately and effectively than from the ground, and to effect rescues from tall buildings. These two jobs were essential when hand pumps and steamers were plying the streets of 19th-century cities, and 150 years later, they still are.

Developments continued throughout the 1980s and '90s. In 1981, the Grampian Fire Brigade in Scotland ordered a Metz DLK30 electro-hydraulically powered turntable ladder mounted on a Scania chassis. The ladder could reach 100ft (30m), the platform at its head supplied with

electricity for power tools and floodlighting, with the current provided by a 110V generator mounted on the turntable. Like all modern aerials, it had a jacking system to keep the appliance stable while the ladder was at its full extent, and it was the first in the UK to be continuously monitored by a computerized fault-finding diagnostic display.

A further advance in jacking technology appeared in 1991 in another Metz turntable, the DLK30 PLC, 'PLC' standing for Programme Logic Control, which allowed variable-width and electronic ground-pressure control, the latter being a useful feature in the event of the appliance having to operate from soft ground rather than tarmac or concrete. At the time, this was also the only turntable ladder with both powered lowering and elevation, which allowed it to be depressed to 24 degrees below the horizontal. The aerial size when folded was more of an issue on Britain's narrower roads than in the USA, and an earlier ladder by German manufacturer Magirus was promoted as offering a travelling height

A four-stage aerial ladder with mid-mounted pump.

of only 9ft 4.5in (2.85m), which was of real benefit when accessing restricted areas.

Today, the major American manufacturers offer turntable ladders on their custom chassis. Pierce, for example, has ladders of 75, 100 or 105ft, in aluminium or steel. The 75-ft (23-m) version, mounted over the rear wheels, has a horizontal reach of 66ft, and a rated load of 500lbs (225kg), while delivering 1500gpm from the ladder-mounted nozzle, or 750lbs (340kg) when operating dry. Powered by dual hydraulic cylinders, in both elevation and retraction, the ladder can be raised from 5 degrees below the horizontal to 80 degrees above. All the

ABOVE: A specialist ladder-only appliance, with rear-mounted turntable.

OPPOSITE: Note the yellow monitor mounted on the ladder set-up.

hydraulic cylinders have integral holding valves that prevent them from losing pressure in the event of an hydraulic line failure. There is also a 12V emergency power unit, should the electrics fail, capable of supplying for up to 30 minutes, and which has enough juice to retract and stow the ladder should the need arise.

When fully extended, the ladder is stable in up to 40-mph (64-km/h) winds

and with a coating of up to a quarter-inch of ice, the ice issue being an important one in turntable ladders in particular. Not only does it make the ladder tricky to climb, but the weight of encrusted ice adds considerably to the ladder's load or, more to the point, reduces the load capacity for firefighters and rescue victims. Like all ladders, this not only acts as a water delivery system, but also as a rescue

device, with the top-mounted water monitor able to swivel through 180 degrees. It is supplied by a telescoping aluminium waterway capable of moving 1000gpm, itself supplied by a 4-in (102-mm) base pipe. There is, of course, a wide choice of pumps, either midship-mounted or driven from a power take-off. In the case of the former, Waterous, Hale or Darley pumps are offered in 500–2000-gpm

sizes, while the PTO pumps deliver from 250–1000gpm.

The basic 75-ft ladder is available on all of Pierce's custom chassis, including the Velocity, Impel, Quantum and Arrow XT. It is also rear-mounted, as are most of the company's turntable ladders, but a mid-mounted ladder of 100ft (30m) is also available. Extendable in five sections, this has a capacity of

750lbs, and Pierce claims it has one of the lowest travelling heights in the business, it being also capable of withstanding a 50-mph (80-km/h) wind.

The ladder is mounted to a torque box subframe behind the cab, and the whole appliance is steadied by two sets of H-style stabilizers; as ladders have got taller, with ever wider horizontal reaches, appliances have needed these

extra stabilizers, the H-style being more heavy duty than basic side stabilizers, and are able to establish a wider base. On some of Pierce's ladders, such as the

ABOVE: They appear to do things differently in the Bayou.

OPPOSITE: Newport's aerial ladder, with rear turntable and midship pump.

75- and 100-ft heavy-duty models, the H-style stabilizers reach out to 16ft (4.9m), with a short-jack capability of 12ft (3.6m) where space is tight. Pierce's mid-mounted ladder is on a different scale from the 75-ft rear-mounted device described above, in that it has an hydraulic-fluid reservoir of 70 gallons as opposed to 38 gallons in the 75-ft.

If Pierce Manufacturing, being one of the oldest names in the US fire engine business, supplies a range of turntable ladders, what about one of the newest, Ferrara? Chris Ferrara's company prides itself on offering five different lengths – 57, 77, 100 and 107ft,

together with a sky-scraping 127ft (38.7m). It's interesting to note that although buildings have become significantly taller in the past 50 years, turntable ladders have not, there being a practical limit to the height that can be transported through city streets and still remain stable when fully extended.

All of Ferrara's ladders are rear-mounted, and they are offered in standard or quintuple (quint) forms. If in the latter (which means the appliance is equipped to perform five major tasks) the pumper side of the equation is provided by a pump of up to 2250gpm or as little as 250gpm. The big 127-ft

ladder can take a 500-lb load while delivering 1250gpm, and offers a 180-degree nozzle sweep. The nozzle is supplied by a telescopic tube of chrome-plated steel, which Ferrara maintains is more durable than aluminium for this particular purpose, and which needs less maintenance. The ladder itself is raised from 8 degrees below horizontal to 72 degrees above, and at zero degree can reach out horizontally to 101ft.

Reassuringly, it is strong enough to operate like that, in that there is an 8-ft (2.4-m) overlap between each of the five sections, meaning that what the ladder loses in height it gains in strength and

stability. But it still has a load-sensing system that keeps the operator fully informed of the ladder's current load status, particularly useful when there is a build-up of ice on the ladder. As for operator error, and even firefighters are human, a safety interlock prevents the ladder from being rotated into an unstable position, or from hitting the body and cab at low elevations.

SNORKEL BOB

When Chicago Fire Commissioner Robert Quinn hit on the idea of using an hydraulic-boom cherry picker for firefighting, he probably had no notion

of what he'd started. The equipment proved ideal for both firefighting and rescues, with a secure platform able to hold a couple of firefighters to tackle the blaze or lower up to six people to

safety. Having been based on existing technology, it was quickly adaptable to its new purpose, and the 'snorkel' soon became a standard feature of most manufacturers' lineups. As for Quinn, forever more he was known as 'Snorkel Bob'. History does not record what he thought of this, but his contribution to the development of the fire appliance is undeniable.

American manufacturers quickly adopted the idea, and only three years after Snorkel Bob's bright idea, the first British snorkel was unveiled at an industry conference in Edinburgh. It was built by Simon Engineering (Dudley) Ltd., which already made hydraulic platforms for other uses. The demonstrator was a two-boom lift,

reaching 65ft (20m) and with the ability to support a load of 1,000lbs (455kg) on the platform, reaching maximum height in 50 seconds. The first model to go operational also had a water fog device that was able to envelope the cage in moisture, thus keeping the occupants safe from flames and heat.

As with the longer ladders, it was necessary for British manufacturers to make hydraulic platforms more compact to fit the country's smaller twisting roads, and in 1962 Simon Engineering patented a three-boom

LEFT: The mid-mounted turntable gives the ladder more scope.

ABOVE: Note the rear access to the turntable.

platform that reached 85ft (26m) fully extended, but which had a travelling length of only 38ft (11.6m). It was the extra third boom that allowed this long reach, coupled with a relatively compact travelling length.

Simon Engineering became a leader in the UK market, though in 1967 appliance-maker Carmichael began to offer a Swedish Wibe Orbitor hydraulic platform, the largest of which was able to reach 72ft (22m), and outreach to over 35ft (10.7m). Simon responded with the 70-ft (21.3-m) Simon Snorkel the following year, and in 1972 launched the SS289, its highest platform yet, with the capacity to reach 100ft (30m). But the slightly smaller SS263, at 91ft (28m), coupled with a cage capacity of 800lbs (363kg), proved more popular with British brigades. Oil

ABOVE: Most US-built aerial ladders are six-wheelers, as shown here.

OPPOSITE: Ladders have remained the one constant in the history of fire engines,

FIRE ENGINES

refineries ordered Simon's 103-ft SS300 in the late 1970s and early '80s, while 1979 saw the launch of the EPL Firecracker, which used a telescopic upper boom to maintain a compact travelling length.

Some of these hydraulic platforms came with built-in booster pumps, purely to supply the monitor on the platform, and these were known as hydraulic platform pumps, not to be confused with pump hydraulic

platforms, which were proper pumping engines with small hydraulic platforms of maybe 50ft instead of an aerial ladder. Hydraulic platform pumps, on the other hand, were platforms first, pumpers second.

FERRARA:
THE NEW BOY

The firefighting industry has its well-respected and long-established names on both sides of the Atlantic, and companies such as Pierce, Dennis and American LaFrance have been fighting fires for decades – in some cases for 100 years. Compared with these, Ferrara is the new kid on the block, not entering full-scale production until 1988, yet now among the top five US manufacturers of fire engines. How did this happen?

The story starts back in 1977, when Chris Ferrara was working as a pipefitter/fabricator at a large petro-chemical refinery near Baton Rouge, Louisiana. Chris was also a volunteer firefighter with the Central Volunteer Fire Department, and was painfully aware that his local fire department was facing a number of problems, serving a rural area where the water supply was frequently limited. A modern water tanker was the obvious answer, but there were insufficient funds to buy one, so Chris Ferrara decided to make one himself.

He was well-placed to do so, given his previous experience, and with the help of department colleagues he succeeded in building a one-off tanker that saved his superiors thousands of dollars.

This first tanker was destined not to be a one-off, however, for it encouraged Chris to leave his regular job and set up a firefighting equipment and supply distributorship. Established in 1979, Ferrara Firefighting Equipment operated out of Ferrara's home, where it thrived, and three years later the company was officially incorporated, with a full service, warranty and repair centre for several major apparatus manufacturers.

Six years later, in 1988, Ferrara Firefighting Equipment began to build fire engines itself. Starting early in the year, this was initially an assembly operation, mounting pre-built fire bodies and fire pumps onto new and used chassis, which didn't meet the individual needs of many customers, and

within months Chris set up Ferrara Fire Apparatus to build fire engines to its own design, which would eventually include a complete line, mainly commercial pumpers, tankers, mini-pumpers and service/utility vehicles.

It was a massive change for the company, and coincided with an expansion of the refurbishment business. But it worked well, and by 1992 Ferrara found itself ranked as the tenth largest manufacturer of fire apparatus in the USA, with 103 units having been delivered. The transformation from regional distributor/refurbisher to national manufacturer had taken just four years.

The company soon proved itself capable of creating innovations of its own, one of the first of these being its custom extruded-aluminum fire body. Built entirely of aluminium plate and extrusions, this was at the forefront of industry design, saving weight while retaining strength. Ferrara would go on to offer customers a wide range of body materials and constructions, using galvaneel steel, stainless steel, unitary all-welded bodies and extruded aluminium.

Aerial ladders and platforms were added to the range in the early 1990s, and demand for the whole lineup was such that the company moved to a bigger factory in 1994. Located between Baton Rouge and New Orleans, this covered 110,000sq ft (10229m²) and was designed specifically for its purpose around the actual stages of production, and Ferrara claimed it to be one of the most modern plants in the industry.

Throughout the 1990s, the company had been fitting its custom bodies to standard chassis, and the obvious next step was to build its own custom chassis as well. Inferno was the dramatic name given to the first Ferrara chassis, which was unveiled in 1999. There were several advantages in having a new design rather than using an existing truck chassis, in that the custom chassis was likely to be more comfortable, better able to cope with high-speed duties, and be easier to handle. Ferrara claimed all of these advantages for the Inferno, along with more space for the crew, better driver visibility, certified and optimized steering, climate control, safety, and easier maintenance.

A mid-range version, the Igniter, soon followed, with many of the same features, though it may have been a worry to some that Ferrara favoured such fiery names! Whatever the name, a whole range of variations on the theme followed, including the Inferno Lo Cab, Rescue Cab, an all-wheel-drive version, and the Inferno Ultra chassis for extreme conditions. A coil-sprung independent front suspension was added later, as was CAPS (Complete Airbag Protection System), in a bid to further improve the handling and safety of these custom fire engines.

Once again, Ferrara sought expansion to keep up with demand, and 40,000sq ft were added to the factory in 2000 to build more Inferno and Igniter chassis. Five years later, another 10,000sq ft was built on, to be used for yet more chassis-building as well as to continue the service, repair and refurbishment aspects of the business.

Today, Ferrara is an acknowledged leading player in the US, and building up to 330 trucks a year puts it into the top five. It continues to offer a whole range of commercial and custom fire engines with innovative features, which are in service in 35 major cities across the USA, as well as being exported to Canada, Mexico, the Middle East and even China.

The company was responsible for building the first new fire appliance to be donated to New York City after September 11, and 2004 also saw the launch of Strong Arm, a substantial remote-controlled hydraulic arm that could be adapted to a huge variety of tasks, including forced entry, demolition, and crane and foam delivery. All in all, this has been good going for a business that began life saving a small fire department a few dollars.

OPPOSITE: Tradition lingers on in the placing of the chrome-plated bell on the front platform.

ABOVE: There is ingenious hose storage on this aerial.

An example of the pump hydraulic platform was the Simon Snorkel SS50, mounted on a Ford D800 chassis and supplied to the Welsh Monmouthshire Fire Brigade in 1970. This was primarily a pumper, with a rear-mounted Godiva 500-gpm pump and 250-gallon water tank. A later example was the 1993 Scania 6x4 unit, run by Wiltshire, in England, that combined a 49-ft (15-m) reach hydraulic platform with a 500-gpm pump and 220-gallon tank.

AERIALS: SNORKEL BOB & FRIENDS

Yet another variation on the theme of the hydraulic platform is the aerial ladder platform, which combines a platform and ladder in the same unit. The Finnish-made Bronto Skylift 28.2T1 was one such in 1985, with a 97-ft (29.5-m) boom and with an outreach of 59ft (18m); it also had a telescopic rescue ladder running alongside the boom. Some previous platforms had

BELOW: IVECO-Magirus offers a range of aerial appliances.

OPPOSITE: Clever jointing allows platform and hose to extend below the horizontal.

also been fitted with ladders, but purely as emergency escapes in the event of hydraulic failure.

Simon Engineering responded to the Finnish equipment in 1989 with a 100-ft (30-m) aerial ladder platform, the first having been built for the English Yorkshire brigade. Others followed, though the ALP 340 of 1995 proved to be the last before the company closed down. With a telescopic main boom and articulated tip boom, it had a working height of 111.5ft (34m) and was able to drop down to 16ft (5m) below road level.

Today, both Ferrara and Pierce offer aerial platforms as well as ladders, those of Ferrara coming in 85- or 100-ft (26- or 30-m) lengths, both available either rear- or mid-mounted. Mid-

LEFT: A custom-built Magirus with fold-down platform.

ABOVE: When stowed, ladders and platforms must be made as compact as possible.

monitor, though it is double this when it is working dry.

Dual monitors are an option, with up to 2000gpm between them, the boom having the capability of working between 8 degrees below horizontal and 72 degrees above. The platform, which at 21sq ft (1.95m^2) is big enough for four fully kitted-up firefighters, has a couple of interesting features, including pre-piped breathing connectors and a 75-gpm sprinkler for the underside, to protect personnel when working over flames.

mounting the apparatus has considerable advantages, making for a lower travel height and thus lowering the whole appliance's centre of gravity. It also takes up valuable storage space, however, so both companies offer platforms in either mounting point, leaving the choice to individual fire departments. Taking Ferrara's 100-ft rear-mounted as an example, this has a 500-lb load capacity on the platform when delivering 1000gpm through the

LEFT: Floral Park's Pierce appliance, complete with stars 'n' stripes front end.

ABOVE: Monitor triggers must be robust and simple to use.

RIGHT: There is room for two firefighters on this platform, which is extended horizontally.

Pierce offers 85- and 100-ft rear-mounted and a single 95-ft mid-mounted aerial platform, the latter with an impressive travelling height of only 9ft 10in (3m). This is a quint appliance, with a 300-gallon water tank, while the five-section telescoping ladder and self-levelling platform are all electronically controlled. Pierce's flagship in this sector, however, is the Sky Arm, which claims to be the only four-section 100-ft articulating aerial ladder available in the USA. Its important feature is the ability to work up to 60 degrees below road level, making it ideal for rescues from ravines, water and ditches.

But for all the safety precautions, such as self-levelling platforms with built-in breathing supplies and cooling sprinklers, sometimes the conditions are just too dangerous for firefighters to use an aerial ladder or platform, which is when remote-controlled monitors come into their own. These were first seen in the late 1960s, and

ABOVE LEFT: Hydraulic arms can also be used for recovering crashed cars.

LEFT: The hydraulic arm folds neatly away when not in use.

SEAGRAVE: AERIAL EXPERT

*F*rederick Seagrave never intended to build fire appliances at all. Starting out in business in Michigan in 1881, he made ladders for fruit-pickers that were so well-constructed that he was approached by a local fire department to build, not only ladders but also a wheeled platform for hauling them to fire scenes. Soon afterwards, Seagrave went into regular production of horse-drawn wooden ladders, and was so busy that the company had to move to a bigger factory at Colombus, Ohio.

There were, of course, plenty of manufacturers of horse-drawn appliances, and many did not survive, although Seagrave did, due to a talent for having innovative ideas and putting them into production.

Seagrave ladders were now reaching up to 85ft (26m), but raising them was a slow and arduous process, even for four men working hard. It was in around 1900 that someone in the company had the idea of using springs to assist in raising them, which were a great success, helping to consolidate Seagrave's position as one of the leading makers of aerials. In 1935 it launched the world's first all-welded alloy-steel ladder, this being far lighter and with a longer life than the traditional wooden ladder. Soon after, the company introduced the first all-hydraulic ladder, that was both raised and extended by hydraulics, and the format for the modern aerial ladder was born.

But although Seagrave was famous for its aerials, and the innovations surrounding them, it also pioneered other features. It had developed a centrifugal water pump, even before the beginning of the First World War, this

being more efficient than the rotary and piston types. Seagrave also worked on engine cooling systems, a vital feature for engines that would be working hard at the pumps for long periods and with the fire engine stationary.

The company also invented the closed canopy cab in 1937, the basic layout of which would be in production for over 30 years. At a time when just about every other fire engine left its crew exposed to the weather, this was a radical step, and consisted of an enclosed compartment for the officer and driver, with a canopy extended rearwards over a bench seat for three or four firefighters. There were even four-door sedan-style closed cabs, which gave everyone concerned the luxury of full enclosure.

Throughout the 1950s and '60s, Seagrave continued to develop its range of aerials, ladders and pumpers, even though its location was moved after it was taken over by the FWD Corporation in 1964. Naturally, aerials were still a core part of the range, a typical 100-ft ladder being rear-mounted on an appliance powered by a 350-hp (261-kW) Detroit Diesel V6, coupled with a four-speed automatic transmission. As used by the New York Fire Department, these weighed in at 14.5 tons.

Still under FWD ownership, the company continued to thrive into the 21st century, and it was the continuing interest in Seagrave's older appliances that led it to offer an archive service for collectors. Given the serial number for anything built before 1970, Seagrave would do its best to supply the original specifications, photographs and maintenance manuals.

EMERGENCY ONE:
CHAMPION OF ALUMINIUM

Emergency One, better known throughout the US firefighting industry as E-One, demonstrates how open the industry is to new names and new start-ups, and old and respected marques, such as Pierce and American LaFrance, are able to reside alongside newer ones such as Ferrara and E-One. With headquarters at Oscala, Florida, E-One launched its first fire engine in 1974, and to date has built over 2,300, many of which have been exported throughout the world.

This innovative company has always been a strong proponent of aluminium as a building material, and the metal has several advantages over steel. It is certainly more expensive, but is far more resistant to corrosion and thus provides a longer service life. Crucially, aluminium is also lighter, which allows a bigger payload and results in less wear and tear on the power train. As a side benefit, aluminium doesn't need painting, which saves on maintenance bills over the years.

Another of E-One's great ideas, although it was not exactly a new one in industry, was modular construction, which meant that certain sections of bodywork could be prefabricated and slotted together when required, and that

appliances with very different equipment could be based around the same design. This made the whole production process quicker as well as cheaper, and E-One would claim the ability to deliver a new fire engine in only 90 days.

Today, the company is proud to make its own chassis, but it has also built appliances onto Ford, Freightliner and General Motors running gear, an example of the latter being the Midi-Pumper, based on the GM four-wheel-drive running gear and designed for rural fire departments. It had a mid-mounted pump of 750gpm, supplied by a 500-gallon water tank, and with four-wheel-drive could be relied upon to get to fires that other appliances were not able to access.

Following that first aluminium modular fire truck in 1974, the new launches and innovations continued, though the company was taken over by the Federal Signal Corporation in 1979. That same year, a 55-ft (17-m) aerial was launched, with a torque box the following year and a 110-ft (33.5-m) ladder the year after. In fact, E-One would also offer a strong lineup of aerials, and claimed that the 110-ft ladder was one of the highest available at the time. It was part of the Strato Spear range, which also included aerial platforms and telescopic booms. E-One's first aerial platforms were unveiled in 1980, built onto a multi-purpose appliance that could operate as a pumper as well, and launched a 95-ft platform and 135-ft ladder in 1983. The ladders were of welded aluminium, of course, coupled in the Strato Spear range with an underslung jacking system. The company also offered a compact aerial, with a 95-ft ladder on a two-axle chassis.

E-One's position was bolstered when its parent company bought Bronto Skylift, the leading Finnish aerial platform-maker, in 1995, and the Saulsbury Fire Rescue Company was acquired three years later. Although well-known for its aerials, E-One has also built a whole range of other equipment, such as the low-profile Titan HPR foam tender range, offered in 4x4, 6x6 and 8x8 forms.

FIRE ENGINES

Scotland's Glasgow Fire Service began using what were called 'scooshers' in 1969.

The monitor was mounted on top of twin hydraulic booms, supplied by a 900-gpm pump and 200-gallon water tank. The Simon booms had a working height of a little over 31ft (9m), while the Angus Fognozl monitor could be controlled from the ground. It incorporated window-breaking equipment and there was an infra-red detector, giving the ground-based operator an idea of the

LEFT: Ferrara's Strong Arm is able to punch through 6in (15cm) of concrete.

ABOVE: The fog spray pattern delivered by the Strong Arm.

More recently, the American Snozzle has seen service in the UK in the form of the P50 articulated and telescopic boom, first shown in 1995. The 49.2-ft (15-m) boom had a piercing nozzle, originally designed to penetrate burning aircraft, but which also proved capable of breaking through into buildings. Instead of the early remote-control's infra-red detection, this carried lighting and camera systems so that the operator could work the monitor by sight.

Perhaps the ultimate remote-control device is Ferrara's current Strong Arm, which was developed in

whereabouts of the fire. Bigger scooshers followed in the 1970s, based first on 45-ft (14-m) Simon booms with 360-degree movement, and later on 42-ft telescopic booms with 8-ft (2.4-m) ladders, giving a total working height of 50ft (15m).

ABOVE: Strong Arm punches through walls to search out fire.

RIGHT: Remote control makes firefighting a safer business.

OPPOSITE: A three-axle Spartan with large platform.

concert with Gradall, the key to which lies in its hydraulic power, which can exert 40,000lbs (18145-kg) of force at the tip of the articulated boom and in the hardened stainless-steel tip. This can pound its way through most walls and roofs, including 6in (15cm) of reinforced concrete or 3/16-inch of corrugated steel. This 'break and enter' capability means that Strong Arm is able to reach the heart of a fire, and can extinguish a blaze in seconds once contact is made.

Water or foam is delivered through 52 individual aquajet nozzles, while the '5th-Man Nozzle' gives a blanket of foam or a 50-ft-wide curtain of water. Remotely controlled from up to 200-ft (61-m) away, the Strong Arm allows firefighters to keep a safe distance, and besides fighting fires can also act as a crane or controlled demolition device. Few aerials are more spectacular than this when seen in action.

PIERCE:
A FAMILY CONCERN

Pierce Manufacturing is one of the oldest of the established makers of fire engines. Humphrey Pierce and his son Dudley set up in business in Appleton, Wisconsin, back in the 1913. But fire appliances were not their first concern, and the Auto Body Works began by offering truck and bus bodies for the Ford Model T and 1-ton truck chassis. Being a decent base from which to have made a start, the company grew fast, becoming incorporated in 1917, with Humphrey Pierce as its first president. Ten years later, Pierce decided to diversify into the specialized utility market, while at the same time offering standard bodies on Ford and Chevrolet chassis.

It was not until 1940 that Steve Otis asked the company to build a fire truck based on a standard chassis. Otis held the Wisconsin franchise for PTO pumps, making fire appliances a potentially lucrative market. Production began in a small way, with only 20 men turning out one fire engine at a time, but the whole operation moved up a gear when Pierce teamed up with pump-maker W.S. Darley of Rosemont, Illinois. Pierce built pumper bodies equipped

with Darley pumps in an arrangement which worked well, and a substantial order for 41 fire engine trailers was secured from the city of Minneapolis.

The company was quick to spot the potential of the aerial platform, the snorkel, and launching one of these helped annual sales top $1 million for the first time in 1960. At that time, Pierce Manufacturing was still a family-owned business, selling out only in 1967, although the company name, which by now was highly respected, was retained. This was a boom time for Pierce, which saw sales top $2 million that same year. In 1970, a huge new factory covering 62,000sq ft (5760m^2) was built at Menasha, Wisconsin, and five years later a massive order from Saudi Arabia helped to keep it busy, the Saudis having ordered 700 large rescue trucks, trailers and aerials. Pierce was now one of the top three manufacturers of fire engines in the USA.

The company had a long tradition of innovation, and this continued into modern times when it introduced the first aluminium chassis in a bid to reduce weight in 1978. A big USAF order followed, and 1982 saw the company's first custom chassis/cab/body, the Pierce Arrow. Named after the famous car marque, although there was no direct connection between the companies, it was claimed to have changed the face of the industry, setting the style for modern fire trucks with more space and visibility.

More new ideas followed, the 1984 Dash being the first custom tilt-cab in the industry, and the following year the Lance offered a split-tilt cab for the first time. Electronics were creeping into fire engines, as into every other area of life, and 1991 saw the Pierce Micro Controller, a self-diagnostic system monitoring readiness. Five years later, Pierce was the first manufacturer to offer fully integrated multiplexing for simpler troubleshooting. There were new models, too: Saber was claimed to be the first custom chassis offered at an affordable price, while Quantum had the strongest frame in the industry, according to Pierce, while the Husky foam system was able to deliver different foam viscosities at the same time, to suit both Class A and Class B fires.

The year 1998 saw the new Sky Series of aerials, the Sky Arm being the only 100-ft (30-m) articulated aerial ladder platform at the time, while a shorter 85-ft (26-m) platform was integrated with the whole vehicle multiplexing. The following year, Pierce announced a co-operative deal with truck-maker Kenworth, the resulting T-300 having a four-door cab, while the Contender was a complete series of commercial and custom fire engines. The Enforcer was another new custom chassis in 2000, and the company launched a mid-mounted aerial platform with a lower overall height that could operate in high winds.

Safety innovations dominated the early years of the 21st century, notably independent front suspension (2001) and the VLH self-venting discharge cap (2002) which reduced injuries caused by the inadvertent release of pressurized lines. In 2003, the Side Roll Protection System went a long way to

protect the vehicle occupants, the system automatically tightening seat belts, lowering the seats and deploying a tubular air bag in the event of a collision.

Now owned by truck-maker Oshkosh, Pierce Manufacturing was firmly at the forefront of the fire engine industry, and Humphrey and Dudley would have been justly proud.

CHAPTER FOUR

TANKERS:
THE ESSENTIAL BACKUP

Tankers are an essential part of the firefighter's armoury where water supplies are short. Looking at the size of the average pumper's tank, it doesn't take much to work out that when working flat-out, the average-capacity pump will drain it in a minute or less, which does not matter when there are hydrants nearby, or where there is some other source of water, such as a lake or river. But where none is available, there has to be another way, and the purpose-built tanker is the answer.

BELOW & OPPOSITE: Dennis tankers.

PAGES 136–137: A vintage tanker.

There is nothing new about water tankers. Back in 1824, Scotland's Glasgow Fire Brigade was running eight water carts, whose job it was to

transport water from the nearest fire plug to the hand pumps at the scene of a fire. As mentioned in Chapter Two, the British government created a fleet of what were called dam lorries during the Second World War, these being flat-bed trucks with canvas-and-steel 500-gallon water tanks rigged up on the load bed. They were intended to maintain water supplies to pumpers during air raids, when mains water was likely to be disrupted. With the widespread availability of hydrants in cities, towns and suburban areas, the need for specialized tankers is less pressing than it once was, but they are still used in rural areas in both Europe and the USA.

Although modern tankers are purpose-built from new, there have been some interesting conversions. In 1967, the Bedfordshire Fire Brigade in England was faced with the need to provide a fire and rescue service for the

TANKERS: THE ESSENTIAL BACKUP

M1 motorway, that ran through the county, as well as for several small villages lacking in sufficient water for fighting fires.

It drew up specifications for two new 1,200-gallon tankers, but the cost proved to be prohibitive. Some lateral thinking, however, eventually led to the brigade acquiring two secondhand 2,000-gallon petrol tankers, which were converted for fire use by Sun Engineering, with lockers in their side to carry a 2,500-gallon inflatable dam and two portable pumps; a smooth fairing was then added to cover the new equipment. In 1998, and with a large rural area to cover, the Lincolnshire Fire Brigade was able to afford a new

FIRE ENGINES

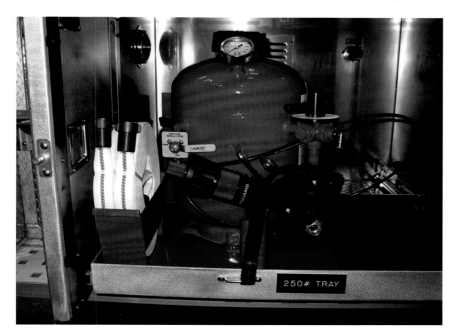

pumper tankers or pure tankers, with stainless-steel or polypropylene tanks plus a huge choice of water-delivery systems. As ever, fire departments are able to tailor the vehicle to their specific needs as far as the budget permits.

Although many tankers are based on commercial truck chassis, such as those from Kenworth, Freightliner and International, others use custom chassis, which in the case of Ferrara brings the option of its coil-sprung independent front suspension. Tankers do not need to be first-response vehicles, but they still need to get to the fire scene quickly and safely, and a fully

purpose-built tanker. Based on a Foden 2215 chassis, the 1,500-gallon tank was supplied by Whale Tankers, with extra bodywork by Warner of Lincoln.

Modern American tankers come in a variety of forms, based on both custom and commercial sizes, as

OPPOSITE: A typical dry-side tanker on a commercial chassis.

ABOVE: Specialist equipment can include compressed gas or air.

RIGHT: A roof-mounted monitor.

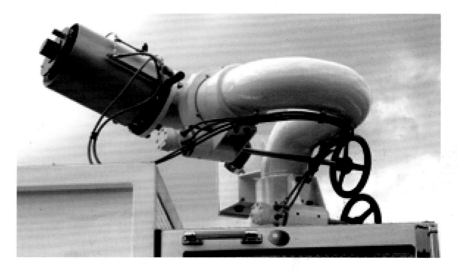

laden tanker benefits from the extra stability afforded by independent front suspension (IFS).

Ferrara claims its coil-sprung set-up is more compact than a torsion bar system, such as that used by Pierce, having 10in (25cm) of suspension travel to absorb bumps and provide more secure handling. Bigger (17-in/432-mm) disc rotors than those on a standard truck suspension give swifter stopping, and the wishbone system with variable spring rates delivers improved handling with less roll. The whole system is designed for ease of maintenance, there being no need for lean adjustments; the hub and pivot bearings are sealed and therefore maintenance-free, and pad replacements can be made without removing the hubs. Finally, with a GAWR of up to 24,000lbs (10885kg), Ferrara's IFS is sufficiently heavy-duty for fully-laden tankers.

ABOVE LEFT & LEFT: There are multiple outlets on these tanker pumps.

OPPOSITE ABOVE: Output can be concentrated...

OPPOSITE BELOW: ... but a wide-ranging fog spray can certainly be impressive.

tanker body, using a formed and welded construction of galvanneal steel, which is the combined process of galvanizing and annealing steel.

Choosing the chassis- and tank-construction is, of course, only the beginning of the process. Ferrara tankers can be equipped as pumpers in their own right, with pumps coming from all the major manufacturers and available in up to 3500gpm, these being midship, PTO-driven and attack or purely transfer pumps. Storage is as much of an issue on tankers as it is on pumpers and aerials, and in this case there is a wide range of options, including enclosed,

These can carry up to 5,000 gallons on a three-axle chassis, and all sizes are offered on Ferrara's custom range as well as the usual commercial choices. The company has long made much of its use of extruded aluminium, which is an option for its tankers, claimed to be the heaviest, strongest and most durable in the industry. The superstructure consists of $7/16$-in heavy-duty twin I-beams, and the body sides and compartments are of $3/16$-in 5052-H3 aluminium plate. An alternative is the modular

ABOVE: A tanker with a mid-mounted pump.

PAGES 144–145: A Pierce Celoron two-axle tanker.

drop-down, electric, overhead, and through-the-tank storage, the latter being a compartment that reaches right through the main water tank. This obviously compromises tank space, but it is a neat solution that leaves the outside compartments free.

Custom Fire offers tankers on commercial chassis only, in both two- and three-axle configurations, with two- or four-door cabs and aluminium or stainless-steel bodywork. These can

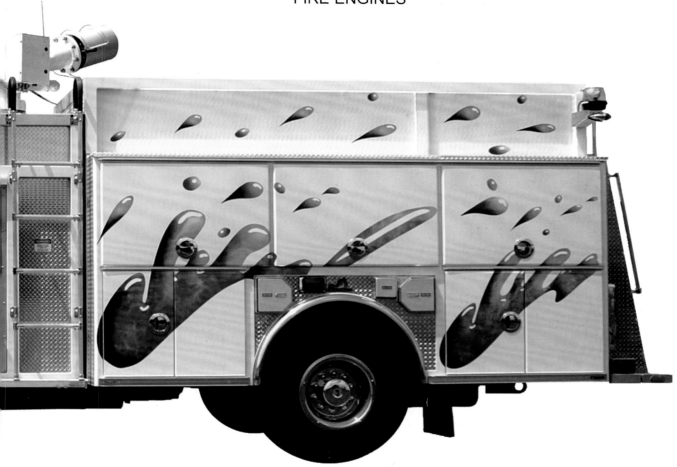

be fitted with slide-in portable tanks, which can be filled on site, plus engine-driven or portable pumps. Where there is no water source close to the fire, portable tanks allow tankers to dump their water load quickly while on site

before making another trip to refill.

Like the other major manufacturers, Custom Fire offers pumper tankers as well as pure tankers, an example of the former being the one delivered to the Edgerton Fire

Department, Wisconsin. It was based on a Spartan Gladiator three-axle chassis, with power coming from a Cummins ISM500 engine driving through an Allison automatic transmission, and came with a

FIRE ENGINES

concealed-bolt stainless-steel body, a FoamPro2001 system, and a Waterous single-stage 2000-gpm pump mounted at the rear. The water tank itself was a relative 2,400 gallons, mid-sized in tanker terms but big enough to make a three-axle chassis essential, with a 30-gallon foam cell as well. To fill the

LEFT: Another dry-side tanker, this time operated by the St. Tammany Parish, Louisiana.

BELOW: A wet-side tanker on a commercial chassis. Note the elliptical tank.

PAGES 148–149: An International Loadstar 1700 tanker.

tank, there were 5-in (127-mm) hard-suction hoses, while discharge was by means of 2.5- and 3.5-in outlets at the rear and passenger sides, plus a top-mounted rear deluge discharge. Other features included a Waterous Oil-Less pump primer and a Class 1 Captain Pressure Governer.

An example of a pure tanker from Custom Fire was the 2,000-gallon machine supplied to the Rockford Fire Department in Minnesota. It was based on a Sterling Acterra chassis, with power supplied by a 300-hp (223.7-kW) Mercedes MBE900, the transmission being an Allison 3000 EVS. It utilized through-the-tank storage, with a portable fold-up tank stored in a sleeve that ran through the main tank. For quick delivery of the load, telescoping dump chutes were fitted at the driver and passenger sides, also at the rear.

Tankers, whether carrying water, fuel or hazardous chemicals, are increasingly using elliptical-shaped tanks, which lower the centre of gravity, thus improving stability and handling of the laden truck. Pierce offers an elliptical tanker on all of its custom

This Kenworth commercial chassis provides a solid base.

chassis – Velocity, Impel, Quantum and Arrow XT – as well as on most commercial chassis, such as Kenworth and Freightliner.

Pierce went to great lengths, when designing the elliptical tank, to eliminate stress points. This is an important issue for tankers, as stresses passed to the tank via the chassis can cause the tank to split and rupture. Pierce has a 'twist test', which involves placing the entire truck on a test rig

OPPOSITE: Firefighters are also called upon to work in snow.

ABOVE: Longshop McCoy's dry-side tanker. Note the tank-level warning lights.

and raising the diagonally opposite front and rear wheels by 9in (23cm) to severely flex the chassis and identify any potential stress points on the tank. The tank itself is of stainless steel, accompanied by a 20-year warranty, or of polypropylene, which is insulated

and comes with a lifetime warranty. E-One also offers a poly tank for its tankers, but one that is encased in stainless steel.

The Pierce tanks come in a variety of sizes from 1,500–4,000 gallons, and in a range of different body designs, all

ABOVE: In Australia, bush fires are a real and present danger.

OPPOSITE: A Pierce tanker: the distinctive extended cab is shared with other Pierce fire engines.

PAGES 156–157: A tanker taking on water from a roadside hydrant.

aimed at optimizing weight distribution and keeping the overall height and centre of gravity to a minimum. Body lengths are 148, 182 or 216in (3.75, 4.6 or 5.5m), including three-axle, and rear dumps of 8, 10 or 12in (20–30cm) are available, with manual, pneumatic or electric valves controlled from the cab.

Jet-assisted dumps are another option, and a 12-in jet-assist can deliver water at up to 3750gpm, so that even the biggest tanker can very quickly jettison its full load and be on its way to collect another.

A Pierce pumper tanker for the Buchanan Valley Volunteer Fire

ABOVE: A smart commercial-chassised two-axle appliance.

OPPOSITE: An FFA (Friendship Fire Association) machine with extended cab and mid-mounted pump.

Department, Pennsylvania, was based on an Arrow XT chassis with TAK-4 independent front suspension and a 515-hp (384.03-kW) power unit. It came with a 2,000-gallon tank, 2000-gpm pump and 13.4-hp (10-kW) generator, plus an 8-in side dump and 10-in rear. This machine was flat-sided, and Pierce offers these 'dry-side' tankers as an alternative to the exposed elliptical ones. The tank is still elliptical, but is enclosed by aluminium side sheets, giving a traditional look and preventing the tank sides from 'sweating'. Otherwise, the specification and options are the same as those for an exposed tank.

Tankers are another example of modern equipment doing exactly the same jobs as their predecessors of a century or more ago, but on a bigger scale. And as long as fires are still fought using copious amounts of water, and occur away from easily tapped supplies, they will remain an essential part of the fire service.

A Fiat 130 tanker of the Suez Fire Brigade.

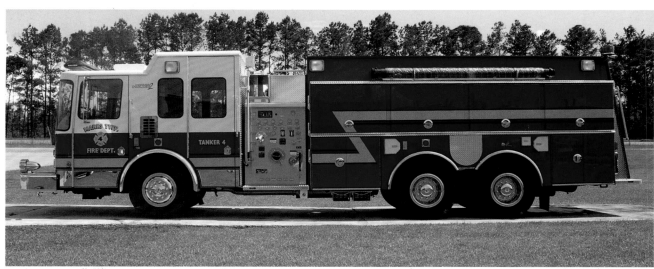

CUSTOM FIRE APPARATUS: A FAMILY AFFAIR

Not many makers of fire engines are able to claim family involvement in a business going back four generations, but Custom Fire is very proud of this very fact. Elmer Abrahamson, the great-grandfather of the current boss, Wayde Kirvida, was a blacksmith who also built a fire truck for his home town of Lindstrom, Minnesota. More engines followed, and a new business was born.

Elmer's daughter married Mitchell Kirvida, who came from Russian farming stock and who joined the now thriving company. They had a son, Jim, who also worked in the family business before striking out on his own and setting up Custom Fire Apparatus.

Incorporated in the late 1970s, Custom Fire began life in a 40 x 40-ft aircraft hangar in Osceola, Wisconsin, with Jim concentrating on building grass rig units, mounted on pickup trucks. His son, Wayde, later recalled that the hangar was too small to paint a rig in one go, so it had to be done in two halves! That problem was solved in 1982, however, when the city of Osceola persuaded Jim Kirvida to buy a vacant aircraft factory nearby. 'The building was much larger than he needed, according to Wayde. 'It was so big, that when he moved the shop in, there was still plenty of room for Jim and his friends to race cars around inside.'

But Custom Fire was still a tiny company compared with the industry giants, though it was given a boost when Waterous pumps made it an approved manufacturer, which allowed the company to supply key fire department customers in St. Paul, the twin city suburbs and Wisconsin. Another boost came in the form of the Full Response cab, launched in the late 1980s, which accommodated all the firefighters inside a safe structure.

When Custom Fire was setting up, the word 'custom' wasn't used widely in the fire appliance industry. Now, it's a byword, but back in the late 1970s most manufacturers simply offered a line of standard models with a fixed range of options. Custom Fire aimed to be more flexible, trying to build exactly what each department needed rather than persuading them to adapt to a standardized design. In fact, it even built a cab to fit the heights of the firefighters who would be using it!

Meanwhile, Wayde was working his way into the company, first helping out during school vacations by sweeping floors and later making deliveries and attending shows. Once an engineering degree from Marquette had been obtained, he worked at Waterous in St. Paul for a while, before returning full-time to Custom Fire in 1998.

The company itself was now offering ever more sophisticated machines, and claimed to have pioneered the use of electronic valves, plus stainless steel for bodies and crew cabs. What it didn't do as a company was to allow itself to get much bigger, and even today Custom Fire employs only 35 people, who between them build 30 to 35 fire engines a year, together with rebuilds.

The company makes bodies only, but prides itself on the fact that they are all bolted together, rather than welded, which allows it to mix construction materials, choosing the right metal for each particular job. Plenty of thought has to go into design as well as construction. Financial constraints mean that many fire departments are seeking to combine different functions in one truck, so that fewer firefighters are required. Moreover, the US appliance market is a competitive one, with around 75 builders competing for about 5,000 orders a year, about half of which are swallowed up by the three or four largest players.

Even so, there continues to be a space in the market for premium fire trucks, and Wayde Kirvida freely admits that Custom Fire trucks aren't the cheapest on the market; but then custom-building never was.

CHAPTER FIVE
THE SPECIALISTS: CRASH TENDERS, FOAM TENDERS, COMMAND CENTRES

Fire engines have many specialized roles, all of them requiring different attributes from those of the basic pumper. Airport crash tenders, for example, need to be fast to reach the ends of long runways in the minimum amount of time. They must deliver foam, rather than water, to deal with the flammable fuel of aircraft fires, and to cope with ever larger aircraft, such as the Boeing 747, they have to be big machines themselves, sometimes massive eight-wheelers from manufacturers such as Rosenbauer and Carmichael.

In the early days of civil aviation, airport tenders were no more than conventional fire engines, modified to produce foam, or light vehicles carrying portable foam extinguishers. Water is generally ineffective when fighting fires involving quantities of flammable

OPPOSITE: A specialist 6x6 airport crash tender, based at Macau Airport.

ABOVE: A commercial-based Rosenbauer, photographed through glass at Geneva Airport in Switzerland.

PAGES 166–167: The Protector, as a specialist airport tender, dispenses foam.

liquids, in that it sinks below the surface of such liquids before it has a chance to cool the fire. Foam, on the other hand, with its bubbles of carbon dioxide, floats on the surface and smothers the fire that more effectively.

Foam was first demonstrated as a firefighting tool as early as 1904, and

was being produced by the Foamite Firefoam Company in 1918. Other foam-makers sprang up on both sides of the Atlantic with names such as 'Fire Suds', 'Fire Froth', and even the poetic 'Fire Snow'. A chemical reaction produced the foam from two concentrates, and on an early

appliance, 220 gallons of the substance produced about 1,760 gallons of foam. Merryweather and Tilling-Stevens were offering specific foam tenders by 1924, and portable foam-making generators eventually followed.

Meanwhile, civil airports were being built requiring their own fire appliances. Equipped with foam tanks, these soon made the transition from the original adaptations of conventional

ABOVE: A high-pressure nozzle dispenses foam.

RIGHT: Bigger runways demand bigger appliances.

FIRE ENGINES

Giant aircraft need bigger fire engines to cope with potential fires.

pumpers. In 1932 the John Morris 'Suvus' tender was adopted as a standard type after it had been used successfully at an air crash in Manchester, England. It carried a 30-gallon foam tank, which allowed a spray of 70ft (21m), and a dozen one-gallon foam containers were on board to bolster up the supply. According to the maker, it could also speed across rough surfaces at up to 50mph (80km/h) in all weathers, which was essential when runways were covered in grass rather than tarmac. Its other rescue equipment was less sophisticated, and included asbestos blankets, a 16-ft (5-m) preventer hook, and various demolition and cutting tools. Asbestos suits were also worn in the 1930s, allowing firefighters to enter burning planes to rescue trapped passengers, even though they were awkward, cumbersome and extremely hot; it was thought that two minutes was the maximum safe period for wearing one.

Twenty years later, and the technology hadn't changed that much; now, a typical airport crash tender carried up to 500 gallons of water and 100 gallons of foam compound. The Thornycroft Nubian, with four-wheel-drive (later versions had six-wheel-drive and a Rolls-Royce eight-cylinder petrol engine) delivered foam at 3500gpm for 1.5 minutes when both of its mechanical foam generators were in operation. It also carried carbon dioxide in six 50-lb (23-kg) cylinders connected to two 100-ft (30-m) hose-reels. An advance in the 1950s was to allow the replenishment of both water and foam supplies without interrupting the delivery of either.

Rescue equipment was also being developed at the time, and separate rescue tenders were often used in tandem with the foam pumper, together with tools such as 12-in electric saws or compressed-air powered saws, plus more breaking, cutting and lifting gear. In the 1970s, smaller rapid-response crash tenders became more popular, which were able to reach the crash site first and contain any fire until the major tender arrived. But even the big machines were expected to get on site quickly, this being a more demanding requirement as runways were lengthened to accommodate larger aircraft. Runways were now surfaced with tarmac, which made higher speeds possible, though airport crash tenders still had four- or

six-wheel-drive in the event of them having to divert off the runway.

In Britain, the Carmichael Jetranger and Scammell Nubian Major 2 were typical examples, both offered in 4x4 and 6x6 configurations. The Scammell was rear-engined, while the Carmichael had its engine behind the front axle, along with a low-profile chassis and water tank to produce a

ABOVE: Rosenbauer's Panther resembles something out of *Thunderbirds*, the TV series of the 1960s.

OPPOSITE: A driver's eye view from the Panther 4x4.

FIRE ENGINES

OPPOSITE: 4x4 and 8x8 Panthers, seen from the cab of a 6x6.

BELOW: In action: a two-axle appliance directs twin foam jets at its target.

low centre of gravity. The Gloster Saro Javelin was another example from the mid 1970s, with a water-tank capacity of up to 2,200 gallons and foam of up to 265 gallons, delivered at 10,000gpm. It used a Reynolds Boughton 6x6 chassis, powered by a General Motors V12 engine and automatic transmission, while later Javelins used a 600-hp (447.4-kW) V16 diesel. A smaller airport tender from a few years later was the Reynolds Boughton RB44 Apollo 4x4 chassis, used as a basis for several rapid-response vehicles. Both Carmichael and HCB-Angus built examples of these on the Apollo chassis.

Back in 1967, the Crash Rescue Equipment Service Incorporated had been established in Dallas, Texas, purely to service and maintain aircraft rescue and firefighting equipment (ARFF). But the company became world-famous thanks to the Snozzle,

the principle behind which was quite simple. Mounted on an elevating extendable boom, it allowed the firefighting nozzle to be placed through small openings in a crashed aircraft, or even pierce the fuselage, spraying foam inside. The Snozzle was also remote-

ABOVE: Based in Berlin, this 6x6 stands ready for work.

OPPOSITE: Rosenbauer appliances are used throughout the world.

PAGES 178–179: Ground-directed water sprays are used to protect the fire engine itself.

FIRE ENGINES

controlled from the cab of the tender, making the whole process safer for the crew. It continues to work as a vital piece of equipment at major airports all over the world, even though it is an expensive item.

Faun-Werke, of Nuremberg, Germany, was particularly notable for large crash tenders built during the 1970s. One of these, the LF1410/52V was one of the biggest fire engines in the world at the time, weighing 50 tons.

It was powered by a 1000-hp (745.7-kW) Daimler-Benz V10 diesel engine, coupled with a four-speed automatic transmission which, despite its prodigious weight, still allowed it to reach 62mph (100km/h) in a little over

a minute. The firefighting equipment, supplied by Metz, was on a similarly massive scale, and included a 4,000-gallon water tank and 440-gallon foam tank. The foam monitor was roof-mounted, by then standard in crash

tenders, but which was an idea that had first appeared back in the mid-1950s.

National Foam of Exton, Pennsylvania, has produced more modestly sized airport crash tenders, drawing on the company's long-

ABOVE: On a four-axle machine, twin steering aids manoeuvrability.

OPPOSITE: Rosenbauer's Panther range.

180

FIRE ENGINES

established specialization in foam appliances, and has supplied equipment to Feecon (Foam Concentrates), while Oshkosh, on the other hand, with its

own background in heavy-duty all-wheel-drive trucks, produces tenders at the other end of the scale. Its current largest model is the M23, its twin

Detroit Diesel engines mustering 984hp (733.9kW) between them, and driving eight wheels via two automatic transmissions. The M23 is a massive

machine weighing 65 tons, and not suprisingly has a correspondingly large capacity, this being 5,000 gallons of water and 430 gallons of foam concentrate, its roof-mounted monitor delivering 2500gpm. Due to the two big diesels, however, the M23 is still able to sprint to its 50-mph (80-km/h) maximum in less than a minute. Oshkosh also offers the smaller M15, with a 900-gpm pump and a mere 4,000-gallon water capacity.

ABOVE: A Panther 8x8 in Turkey.

OPPOSITE: Hydraulic legs keep the vehicle stable.

FIRE ENGINES

Rosenbauer of Austria is a major producer of airport crash tenders (see page 192), with Ziegler of Germany yet another big name in this field. The company, founded by Albert Ziegler back in 1890, is actually the biggest producer of fire engines in the country. It built its first airport crash tender in 1969, and currently offers a whole range of products, from fast-response light rescue vehicles to massive eight-wheelers. Typical of the smaller Zieglers is the VRW, based on either a Mercedes-Benz 412D or Chevrolet Suburban engine, the latter with a 250-bhp V8.

But big airports need big tenders, and for these, Ziegler offers an eight-wheeler to compete with Faun, Rosenbauer and Carmichael. The FLF 60 Z8 weighs 38 tons and carries 2,666 gallons of water, 330 gallons of foam concentrate and 1,100lbs (500kg) of dry powder. Its pump delivers up to 1540gpm, with 1100gpm through the main roof-mounted monitor and 220gpm through the smaller front-mounted monitor, both of which are remote-controlled from inside the cab. As for performance, the big Ziegler is one of the fastest-accelerating of the giant crash tenders, its 1000-bhp MAN V12 pushing out up to 50mph in around 20 seconds.

HOSELAYERS

Hoselayers are a particularly specialized form of fire engine, often with no firefighting capabilities of their own, but they are an essential part of the team where there is no nearby fire hydrant, or where the water source is too far away to be utilized by a conventional pumper. During the Second World War, Britain's National Fire Service operated four-ton trucks

A Rosenbauer in its natural habitat.

A Magirus Super Dragon 8x8.

that carried 6,000ft (1830m) of hose. This was often operated by hand, but more recent hoselayers had the lines neatly stowed, or 'flaked', so that they could be paid out over a ramp at the rear while the vehicle drove at speeds of up to 30mph (48km/h). To cope with the movement of other vehicles over the long lines of hose, hoselayers carried small ramps to enable them to cross the lines without damaging them.

In 1991, the Buckinghamshire Fire & Rescue Service in England took delivery of a four-wheel-drive hoselayer, built by Cambers Engineering of Waddesdon. Based on a IVECO-Ford TurboDaily, this was a light vehicle that nonetheless carried 1.25 miles (2km) of hose, and which was able to lay it across rough terrain that was inaccessible to larger, heavier machines.

Two years later, the Northamptonshire brigade bought a hoselayer with a motorized drum, utilizing the Angus Fetch hose retrieval system, in which an hydraulic lift picked the hose up, retrieved it, and the drum reflaked it into the hose bed. The West Sussex brigade took delivery of a much larger hoselayer in 1998, based

on a 6x4 Mercedes-Benz 2524 25-tonne chassis. Equipped with 1.49 miles (2.4km) of 6-in (150-mm) hose, it came with two Hannay hydraulically-powered drums that were able to lay the hose down at up to 10mph (16km/h). The integrated system also provided powered retrieval, with a closed-circuit screen that allowed the whole operation to be monitored from the cab.

COMMAND CENTRES

The need has always existed for on-site command centres or control units at major fires or crash sites; this is so that the numbers of appliances and firefighters can be accounted for, that it can be known what the firefighters are doing and whether or not they are safe, and so that an overall view of how the incident is being tackled can be established. One might think that in the age of computers, with instant communications and where massive amounts of information can be downloaded in seconds, overseeing an operation from brigade headquarters would be just as effective. But this is not the case: for a fire chief, being on-

A commercial-chassised Magirus based in Germany.

FIRE ENGINES

site and speaking face-to-face with other officers is still the best method of keeping control of an incident.

Not that command centres have always been high-tech. In Britain, in 1949, the Kent Fire Brigade converted a 1931 Leyland Titan double-decker bus to act as a mobile control unit. It wasn't exactly rapid-response, but it was able to take fire alarms and was in telephone contact with brigade headquarters, while radio communications were added later. The bus also acted as a mobile canteen, and came with six bunks, a rest room and washing facilities.

Modern command centres have moved on considerably since then, but their job of supervision and co-ordination is unchanged. Once set up on site, the centre has to log in appliances and crews, and therefore has to be highly visible and distinct from normal appliances, a flashing beacon being a favourite means of accomplishing this.

Effective command is all about information: before the days of the worldwide web, command centres would hold maps and plans detailing water supplies and premises at risk from fire. Now, of course, all of this

information can be downloaded from brigade headquarters to a computer in the on-site command centre. Use is also made of closed-circuit televison and video recording, so that the fire commander can see what is happening at various points on the site.

With all the extra equipment on board, command centres have become larger, an example being the IVECO-Ford Eurocargo chassis delivered to the Bedfordshire brigade in 1994. With bodywork by G.C. Smith, this was divided into three areas, the front cab acting as the communications centre, with a command area in the centre and a conference centre at the rear. As crews checked in on arrival, each firefighter's individual barcode was scanned in, recording their specialist skills, and even any previous exposure to radiation or chemicals. The information superhighway has certainly come to be of great value to the modern task of fighting fires.

A fully extended command centre.

ROSENBAUER: THE HIGH-TECHNICIAN

Today, Rosenbauer is one of the leading manufacturers of high-tech fire engines. It is also one of the largest exporters in the industry, with plants not only in America and Asia but also in Europe producing over 14,000 vehicles a year, which makes it, by any standards, one of the world's major players.

But Rosenbauer is also one of the oldest-established of the manufacturers, Johann Rosenbauer having set up the 'Trading House for Fire Brigade Equipment' in 1866. The company built its first extension ladder in 1870 and went on to produce a series of steam-driven, then petrol-driven pumpers. Throughout the 1920s, a variety of petrol-powered fire engines emerged from the Austrian factory, often using Fiat or Steyr truck chassis. But they weren't all truck-based, and Rosenbauer also offered motorcycle and sidecar outfits such as the Triumph-based 'Little Florian', which could deliver 55 gallons of water per minute. A 10-hp (7.5-kW) portable pump was another product of the 1920s, and in fact portable pumps would still be in the lineup 80 years later.

But the real pointer towards Rosenbauer's future as an appliance-maker lay with the six-wheeled service vehicle of 1930. Based on a Tatra chassis, this was a massive machine that could cross rough terrain, and it was followed up with a foam/water engine-driven pump in 1933.

The company would build many conventional fire engines after the Second World War, but concentrated increasingly on specialist machines with all-terrain ability. It would use chassis from a whole variety of sources, including Mercedes, Scania, Ford, Chevrolet, Steyr, Renault, Faun, Henschel and OM. Of the Ford-based trucks, a typical example from the early 1950s was the water tender built onto a German Ford

V8 4x4 chassis. This came with a 330-gallon water tank and a front-mounted 330-gpm pump.

Rosenbauer's long association with airport crash tenders began around this time, when a crash/foam tender was built for Vienna Airport, based on a 4x4 chassis powered by a Saurer 6GAF-LL diesel engine, and with an 880-gallon tank. From the 1960s Rosenbauer would spend much time designing and building aircraft rescue and firefighting vehicles (ARFFs) specifically for airport use. These grew in size as the years went by, and the first large ARFFs were delivered to Tunis Airport in 1965.

Ten years later, the company announced the SLF18000 Foam truck, based on a Tatra 8x8 chassis, with an 816-hp (608.5-kW) power unit, a 3,080-gallon water capacity, and a top speed of over 60mph (96.5km/h). This rapid increase in capacity and performance reflected the need for airport tenders to be able to reach crash sites as quickly as possible, and to match the size of ever-larger aircraft.

Still bigger was the flagship of the Panther range, this being a complete lineup of 4x4, 6x6 and 8x8 chassis, either from MAN or Freightliner, the largest of these being the Panther 8x8 based on a MAN 38,100 DFAEG chassis with a 1000-hp (745.7-kW) diesel engine. This allowed acceleration to 50mph (80km/h) in 24 seconds and a top speed of around 87mph (140km/h) – astonishing figures for such a large vehicle that tipped the scales at over 38 tons. The 8x8 Panther had a 1540-gpm pump, and a roof monitor that could deliver 1320gpm.

Of course, not all Rosenbauers were built on this scale, and the company also made smaller machines such as the Mercedes-based TSF, with a 4x4 chassis and 143-hp (106.6-

kW) petrol engine. Another example was a forest fire engine, using a Toyota Hi-Lux chassis, that carried 440 gallons of water and 44 gallons of foam concentrate. The company also pioneered the use of demountable pods based on flatbed lorries, so that a wide choice of equipment could be fitted to one vehicle, depending on the emergency it was about to face.

Other later innovations included a new aluminium superstructure in 1994, tunnel fire engines adapted to run on railway tracks in 1999, and a range of articulated aerials in 2004. The following year, a second generation of Panther airport tenders demonstrated that Rosenbauer was more than aware where its core market lay.

CHAPTER SIX

OFF-ROAD:
WILDLAND, FOREST & BRUSH TRUCKS

If the world were perfect, fires would not occur at all, and if they did, they would always be in places easily accessible by means of well-surfaced roads free from traffic congestion. In the real world, however, fires are just as likely to occur in remote areas, far from places where there are roads at all, which is why there is a special group of fire engines that can travel over rough terrain.

In Britain, one of the earliest of these was the Land Rover. The

BELOW: A specialist 4x4 pumper from Canterbury in New Zealand.

OPPOSITE: Rosenbauer's 4x4 fire trucks are able to cope with rough terrain.

potential of this small four-wheel-drive vehicle – Britain's answer to the Willys Jeep – as a light firefighting vehicle soon became obvious to several brigades, and in 1949, only a year after the Land Rover was first introduced, the Derbyshire Fire Service ordered four. These were not equipped as fire engines, but were intended to carry men and equipment across country to where they were needed, towing a trailer pump if necessary.

Rover itself recognized this potential new market, and at the 1952 Commercial Motor Show unveiled a fully-equipped version. One was acquired by the Windsor Castle brigade the following year, equipped with a Pegson 200-gpm pump, a 40-gallon first-aid tank, a 120-ft (37-m) hose-reel and a 35-ft (11-m) alloy extension ladder. Car-maker Austin launched the Champ, its rival to the Land Rover that same year, and in 1956 the Cornwall Fire Brigade bought a Champ chassis, converting it into a light pumper. The Champ was followed by the Austin Gypsy, this too being a candidate that was ripe for conversion. It worked well with the Coventry Climax ACP, which was designed for front mounting, this being a single-stage centrifugal pump rated at 500gpm when operating at 100psi.

The City of Coventry Fire Brigade bought a Land Rover in 1964, though not for its off-road capabilities. The basic short-wheelbase Land Rover was a small, manoeuvrable machine, and the brigade chose it with multi-storey car parks in mind, realizing that a fire

This forestry department 4x4 is able to gain access to difficult areas.

high up in one of these would be inaccessible to a conventional pumper. In this case, the little Land Rover was converted by Carmichael, which fitted a rear-mounted 500-gpm Coventry Climax pump, a 40-gallon tank, and a 120-ft hose-reel, plus a ladder. There was also a front-mounted power winch.

Carmichael, of course, was famous for its six-wheeled Range Rover 6x4s, and although they were often used as airport crash tenders, one also saw service in the rural county of Somerset, in the south-west of England. In 1991, the Range Rover was replaced by a Steyr-Puch-Pinzgauer 718K, a 6x6 machine that was powered by a Volvo 2.4-litre diesel. It was not a factory product, having been converted by Saxon Sanbec, the UK-based manufacturer that ceased production in 2005.

In this case, it was equipped with a GP1600 pump and 110-gallon tank. The cab was able to accommodate five firefighters, and a 33-ft (10-m) triple extension ladder was carried on the roof. Somerset wasn't the first to spot the Saxon Pinzgauer's potential, the first having been bought by the Isle of Man Fire Brigade in 1989, only a few months after it first appeared,

this version carrying a 300-gpm pump. Interestingly, the machine's list price included a training course for the driver.

Britain's Land Rover had been inspired by the Jeep, which itself has been the subject of countless firefighting conversions. Many American companies offered such conversions in the 1950s and beyond, including the Hicks Body Company, W.S. Darley, and the Central Fire Truck Corporation, and post-war conversions were made to thousands of war-surplus Jeeps – both Willys MBs and Ford GPWs – that came onto the civilian market following the Second World War. Once these supplies had dried up, however, post-war production CJ-2As, 3As and 3Bs were given the same treatment, some of them being transformed into aiport crash tenders.

Later, Jeep CJ-5s, -6s, -7s and -8s were all converted for firefighting. In 1982, the Milford Fire Department replaced its war-surplus Jeeps with two CJ-7s, with modifications that included water tanks, radiator shields and Ramsey winches. But the firefighting

A Brea Fire Department Ford F550 with off-road capabilities.

Jeeps were not only chosen for their off-road capability (though of course this came in useful), but some were also converted because their small size meant they could access places that conventional truck-sized fire engines could not. The Wildwood City Fire Department was responsible for a long stretch of ocean-front boardwalk, which was too narrow for a large appliance to access. Consequently, it acquired a Jeep CJ-8 Scrambler in 1996, which wasn't a new idea for Wildwood, the Scrambler having replaced a 1956 Willys. Likewise, the Colonie Fire Company in New York State had a CJ-7 converted in 1983 by Tyler Fire Equipment, this being well-furnished with a 100-gallon water tank, a 500-gpm pump, 250ft (76m) of 1-in (25mm) booster hose, 300ft of 1-in forestry hose, 100ft of 1.5-in attack hose, and a two-way radio. The CJ-7's attraction for the Colonie was that it was small enough to access footpaths and bike trails.

The size issue also applies, though to a lesser extent, to the German-built Unimog, though here its big selling point for firefighters is its ultimate ability to cross rough terrain. As the publicity points out, the quickest way

to a wildland fire often is not by road or even by unsurfaced track, but directly across country. The Unimog is one of the off-road market's perennials, having been launched back in 1948 by Mercedes. It was originally intended as an all-round working vehicle – part tractor, part truck – with four-wheel-drive and huge adaptability. Sixty years later, and its descendants are still being produced as the square-bonneted U3000/4000/5000 and snub-nosed U300/400/500.

The original Unimog was a basic working vehicle, but today the specification reveals a high-tech off-road machine. The U500 is powered by a 6.4-litre six-cylinder diesel, turbo-intercooled to produce 231 or 279hp (172.2 or 208kW). There is permanent four-wheel-drive, and the transmission has eight forward speeds and six reverse, this being an electro-pneumatic unit that comes with Electronic-Quick-Reverse (EQR), the latter allowing the Unimog to be rapidly rocked backwards and forwards to escape when bogged down.

Long-travel coil-sprung suspension, axle articulation of up to 30 degrees, and 20in (501cm) of ground clearance give the Unimog a

tremendous ability to pick its way over rough ground, while the relatively short wheelbase, with minimal overhang, gives it an impressive approach angle of 46 degrees and a departure of 51; it can also ford up to 4ft (1.2m) of water and climb a 45-degree slope. There are differential locks front and rear, the brakes being dual-circuit ABS, and there are other heavy-duty details, such as 24-volt electrics, a tilt-cab, and a compressed air auxiliary connection.

With a specification such as this, it is not surprising that the Unimog brush

OPPOSITE: Designed for airports, the Panther series is also able to run off-road.

BELOW: A GMC fire truck with crew cab.

truck should be such a formidable firefighter. A potential problem for such vehicles, however, is that the stress of driving off-road is communicated to the water tank, which can ultimately split. Mercedes claims that the dual three-point mounting system means that the tank remains free from stress, however hard the chassis and

suspension are worked. Tanks have capacities of up to 1,320 gallons, which obviously compromises space for other equipment, with a pump delivering up to 550gpm. A feature the firefighting Unimog shares with some other brush trucks is the use of external sprays,

which keep crew members safe while walking alongside. The sprays can also be directed onto the tyres, keeping them cool and preventing them from being affected by the intense heat, while a roof hatch enables a fire to be fought from inside the cab, in the event of

ABOVE: Could this be the ultimate in off-road mini-pumps?

OPPOSITE: The three-axle ATV can carry two firefighters and a whole load of equipment.

OFF-ROAD: WILDLAND, FOREST & BRUSH TRUCKS

conditions becoming too dangerous to operate outside.

An indication of the Unimog's effectiveness as an off-road firefighter is the frequency with which it is used across the world. Over 1,000 Unimogs are at work in the south of France, mostly U5000 models with 4000- or 6000-litre tanks and cabs for four firefighters. There are another 250 in Spain, where they double up as winter rescue vehicles in mountainous regions, while in Italy, converted Unimogs have been used in fires for over 30 years, a typical example being the U4000 with interchangeable firefighting or winter service equipment; a U5000 is also available with a 5700-litre water tank, up to three hose-reels, and a 240 litres/minute pump delivering at 60bar.

Some firefighting Unimogs, such as those operating in Croatia, are foam-equipped as well, while in the Sudeten in the Czech Republic they must cope with dry summers as well as snow-bound winters. The Australians make good use of the Unimog for fighting bush fires, as do the Americans, the latter often opting for the U500 with a forest or bush firefighting body, which includes a

5000-litre water tank, roof monitor, two hose-reels, and storage for shovels, axes and other equipment.

SMALL TO BIG

All of the above are based on well-known, series-production four-wheel-drives. But there have been several more unusual solutions to the problem of fighting fire off-road. Back in 1971, the Surrey Fire Brigade in England bought an Argocat, this being a small eight-wheeler about 10-ft (3-m) long, and with a plastic body. Its light weight, and its eight low-pressure (2psi) balloon tyres made the Argocat useful as an amphibious vehicle. With each of the eight wheels independently driven, the power coming from a 436-cc two-stroke engine, it could paddle its way through swamps, mud, sand and snow. It was able to carry six men and a portable pump, though there wasn't room for much else given its small size.

The Argocat is no longer in production, but a new company was set up in Scotland in 1988 to produce the Scot-Track. This was built on a similar

Crash Fire Rescue, the most boring job on the flight deck except when disaster strikes! This is a complete fire truck on a very small scale.

scale to the Argocat, being another eight-wheeler, but was more sophisticated, with a cab and the ability to fit tracks over its eight wheels. It could tow a trailer, and stabilizing legs were available, making it suitable for firefighting. The West Yorkshire Fire Service bought a Scot-Track HillCat 1700 in 1998, which was transported using a curtain-side truck.

Modern American brush trucks are on a different scale to any of these, though they still come in a wide variety of sizes. They have all-wheel drive, of course, and are capable of crossing rough terrain; but some are also designed for the urban/wilderness interface, as the makers describe it, these being suburban areas that may involve some off-road operation to get them to the scene of a fire.

FIRE ENGINES

E-One's Flatbed is the smallest of its off-road range, being part of the ClassicFire series. It is based on a Ford F550 two-door pickup, intended to get firefighters off-road and enable them to tackle small bush fires. Powered by a 6.0-litre diesel with a five-speed automatic transmission, the Flatbed has four-wheel-drive, as one might expect; moreover, it really is a flatbed as the name implies.

In place of the normal pickup bed, E-One has fitted an extruded aluminium platform, which carries all the essential equipment, and with no conventional body allows easy access

OPPOSITE: A two-seater buggy converted by Rosenbauer.

BELOW: Land Rover conversions have been around since the 1960s.

PAGES 208 & 209: Small 4x4s, such as this Land Rover, can get to places full-sized appliances cannot reach.

for maintenance. Central to the Flatbed's firefighting equipment is a 400-gallon polypropylene water tank and an integral 50-gallon foam tank. There is a simple 'Sightglass' view to check on the level in the tank, and the pump is a Hale HPX200, powered by a 20-hp (14.9-kW) Honda motor. This delivers 50gpm at 140psi or 200gpm at 74psi, and there's a Hale FoamLogix delivery system as well. Other features include stainless-steel manifold and piping, brush guards, a front winch, and twin hose-reels.

E-One also offer a 1,000-gallon capacity big brother, based on medium-duty chassis from Ford, GMC, International or Freightliner, all of them being part of E-One's standard catalogue though built to order. A less common brush truck was the AM General Hummer, operated by the fire department at Cherry Valley, Illinois. Delivered in 1999, it came with a remote-controlled bumper turret and carried both water and foam.

FIRE ENGINES

Ferrara, another new kid on the block, has its own take on the theme of the light brush truck, and offers a whole range, in 4x2 (not intended for serious off-roading), 4x4 and 6x4 configurations.

With the off-road role in mind, great attention is paid to the angles of approach and departure, the latter being vital for effective performance, it being a measure of the amount of overhang beyond front and rear wheels, which

determines how steep a slope the vehicle can approach or leave without grounding. If the standard angle isn't enough, Ferrara offers an optional 25-degree angle at the rear, by slanting the lower rear body to maximize clearance.

Another interesting option is the front jumpline, which provides a shower nozzle just ahead of each front wheel, allowing a firefighter to walk alongside the vehicle in greater safety. Bumper-mounted water/foam turrets can be remote-controlled from the cab, and other options include a heavy-duty brush guard to protect the body and cab, and 500-lb (227-kg) capacity roll-out trays to make equipment more easily accessible.

These examples from Ferrara and E-One are both relatively small trucks, but there's no reason why a medium-duty truck should not be used off-road as well, at least up to the point where its sheer size becomes a handicap. One of these is the Hawk series from Pierce, designed as initial-attack fire trucks with the ability to reach fires in rough terrain that would be impossible for conventional fire engines. Although based on commercial chassis from the likes of Kenworth, Freightliner or International, the series has a long list of options that make it possible to customize a Hawk to satisfy differing needs.

As well as the Hawk Wildland truck, the Model 62 is a variation intended specifically for the US Forestry Service, while the Model 14 is aimed at other federal and state fire protection agencies. The differences between the three models are small, but the specific range of options available on each is a result of thinking through the situations it is likely to face. For example, only the Wildland is available with air horns, in that it is likely to spend more of its time on the road. The Model 62 operates mostly in forests, so cannot be ordered with petrol-powered generators or portable pump, obviously because it is sensible that there should be no spark ignition engine in the middle of a forest. Nor can the Model 62 be had with the Hercules or Husky foam systems, though other foam systems are available.

The Hawk is offered in two body lengths and several configurations, though the wheelbase varies from 171 to 190in (4.3–4.8m), depending on what base chassis is chosen. For many buyers, the selection of commercial chassis will often depend on the make-up of the rest of their fleet, therefore it makes sense for an agency with a largely Kenworth fleet to choose a Kenworth-based Pierce, for which spares and advice will be readily available. The Hawk has a 20,000-lb (9070-kg) towbar, and Pierce makes much of the fact that access to this hitch is achievable from above, there being no need to crawl around beneath the truck.

All three models have a Darley PTO-driven pump of 500gpm, which is one of many options, with the main pump mounted midships and available as a Waterous, Hale or Darley from 500 to 1000gpm, while alternative PTO pumps are in the 250 to 1000gpm range. The polypropylene water tank is 500 to 750 gallons, a typical foam set-up being the FoamPro 1600 Class A, with a 20-gallon polypropylene tank. And while there may be less storage than in a purely custom-built appliance, the Hawk body is 96-in (2.4-m) wide, providing total storage of up to 190cu ft (5.88m³), depending on other options specified. The compartments measure 12-in (30-cm) deep (upper) and 24-in deep (lower).

The Hawk is one of the biggest off-road fire trucks, but the sheer variety of models that are offered, from the little Argocat upwards, shows just how many different situations a fire engine may be expected to face up to in rough terrain.

The Unimog is used by many fire services as a go-anywhere vehicle.

LAND ROVER:
THE GO-ANYWHERE VEHICLE

*T*he Land Rover was inspired by the Jeep, and was originally intended as a run-about, do-it-all machine for farmers, having selectable four-wheel-drive and the ability to drive off-road as well as on tarmac. But this very adaptability, coupled with a decent towing capacity, meant that the tough little Land Rover also made an excellent base for a lightweight fire engine.

Brigades all over the world recognized this fact and began buying the Land Rover for conversion as a vehicle that could carry firefighting and rescue equipment over rough terrain. The early Land Rovers were quite small, but each were generally fitted with short ladders, hose-reels, built-in pumps, small water tanks and hoses. They were powered by 1.6-litre petrol engines, capable of pushing them along at over 50mph (80km/h) on the road.

The size and performance of these early models meant that their usefulness for firefighting was limited, but steady development by Rover over the decades widened the vehicles' scope, carrying capacity, and performance. An early option was a 2.0-litre petrol engine, while wheelbases were lengthened in stages to a choice of 88 or 109in (2.2 or 2.8m) by 1956. Diesel options also followed, and the Land Rover became available with a modern turbo-diesel unit as well as a petrol V8 engine by the 1990s. It not only grew in size, but the long-wheelbase Defender 110 or 130 could also be converted into very useful light fire engines. These carried more sophisticated equipment than the first Land Rover appliances of 40 years earlier, and could include folding knuckle cranes, winches, roll cages, large polypropylene water tanks, various pumps, and compressed air systems with their own compressors delivering a water/foam mixture.

Neither the original Land Rover nor the luxury Range Rover that followed it in 1970, had been envisaged as firefighters. But the Range Rover also proved ideal in this respect, in fact more so for some applications, due to its powerful V8 petrol engine, long-travel coil suspension and all-round disc brakes, and it was particularly suited to the fast-response role at airports and on motorways.

Range Rover firefighting conversions were offered by several specialists, that by Carmichael being a six-wheeler with a third axle added to increase the payload. The Carmichael 6x4 was also able to carry heavy rescue tools, such as hydraulic cutting and lifting gear, generators, and floodlights.

CHAPTER SEVEN

RESCUE: BEYOND THE FIRE

A striking feature of modern fire engines is the wide variety of specialized equipment carried, each rarely having one purpose, with quad or quint appliances equipped to do four or five different jobs. But there is a limit to the amount of extra kit an appliance can carry; overload it and its ability to tackle its main job, whether it be pumper or aerial, is severely compromised. This is where the rescue truck comes in, its purpose being to support the main appliance, carrying equipment for which it is lacking in space; in fact, it is often more effective to have this equipment concentrated in one vehicle rather than have it spread around among several multi-purpose appliances.

The increased importance of the rescue appliance, or rescue tender, as it is sometimes known, reflects the increasingly wide role of fire brigades and departments. Fire crews are just as likely to be called to a road crash, a chemical spill, or to rescue people from

A specialist Pierce appliance designed for dealing with chemical spills.

a collapsed building as they are to an actual fire, and the rescue tender plays a vital role in all of these situations.

But they are not a recent idea. The first supplied in Britain was delivered as early as 1904, this being a

Merryweather unit commissioned by the Manchester Fire Brigade and drawn by horses. Although a steamer, it

had some advanced features that echo those of modern rescue units, in that the steam engine drove a single-cylinder air pump which supplied air to breathing apparatus for the firefighters. This took the form of a leather mask equipped with a telephone receiver and transmitter, connected by wires running through the air hose to a switchboard on the appliance, enabling the officer to communicate with his men; another modern feature was a generator that supplied eight electric lights, making the unit a truly advanced piece of equipment for its time.

Rescue tenders developed rapidly, with oxyacetylene cutting sets joining the growing list of equipment. Even in their early form, they were capable of cutting through 6in (15cm) of steel, a collapsed girder being a good example of their use. Hydraulic lifting jacks were also proving their worth, and were able to move heavy girders or stonework of up to 20 tons. Other lifting gear included chains and pulleys, and if a rescue tender came with a generator to supply electric floodlights, this could also be used to power tools such as drills and saws.

OPPOSITE & RIGHT: The aftermath of 9/11.

217

Early rescue tenders were often called to the aid of workmen overcome by gas in sewers. The rescue crewmen would be protected by ammonia masks and suits, taking a sewer trolley which could be adjusted to squeeze into the underground pipes and bring victims back into the fresh air.

A development of the mid-1950s was the introduction of hydraulic rescue tools, that were adopted rapidly by British fire brigades and which are now almost universal, proving themselves especially useful for freeing crash victims trapped inside wrecked

ABOVE: A Hazardous Incident Team tender.

ABOVE RIGHT: One of Oklahoma's specialist trucks.

cars. The early kit was based around a manually operated hydraulic pump that could power various tools through a high-pressure hose connection. These included a wedge and spreader to prise impacted metal apart, with extensions to increase the size of gaps, while rams of 6 and 8 tons were used as jacks. Hydraulic cutters were the next advance, introduced by Lukas of

Germany in 1972, which led to more new hydraulic tools such as the Hurst 'Jaws of Life', that was able to cut through and spread apart impacted metal.

OPPOSITE: A multi-purpose rescue tender.

ABOVE: Note the extended cab for personnel on this rescue appliance.

As traffic congestion became an increasing problem in the 1960s, big rescue tenders were often supplanted or replaced by smaller, faster and more manoeuvrable machines, and favourite vehicles for conversion into small rescue tenders in Britain were the Land Rover, Range Rover, sometimes with Carmichael's six-wheel conversion, and Ford's larger A series. Another

innovation at around the same time was the air bag, this being a neoprene bag that could be inflated either by compressed air or vehicle exhaust, one of which was not only able to lift a big truck or open up a collapsed trench, but which could also fully inflate in 60 seconds. It was a good idea, but when it was conceived by the Bedfordshire Fire Brigade, such rescue bags were not

OPPOSITE: A Ferrara appliance in Houston, Texas.

ABOVE: This pumper is equipped with a large number of specialist tools.

available commercially, so it developed one of its own from an original design by a government agency.

By now, road crashes constituted one of the most frequent call-outs for fire brigades, which in Britain effected a name change to 'Fire & Rescue Services', while brigades were the first line of defence as far as rail crashes were concerned, where the heavy cutting and lifting gear would prove to be invaluable. In 1995, the Avon Fire

FIRE ENGINES

Brigade commissioned what it termed a road/rail rescue unit, which was a Renault G300.26D truck equipped with rail guidance gear, allowing it to run not only along roads but also railroad tracks. Intended to operate in fast response to incidents in the Severn Rail

LEFT & BELOW: These appliances make the most of the available space on two-axle machines.

Tunnel, it carried 12.5 tons of equipment, including two Alumi rail-karts and trailers.

A rescue tender for more general purposes was delivered to the Hampshire Fire & Rescue Service in 2001. This was based on a Volvo 13-ft (4-m) chassis, powered by a 230-hp (171.5-kW) diesel engine. Equipment included a decontamination shower, breathing apparatus, heavy-duty hydraulic cutting and spreading tools, high-pressure air lifting bags, chemical/gas suits, and equipment for monitoring gas and radiation. A 21-in (533-mm) diameter positive pressure ventilation fan was also on board to disperse gas and smoke.

Accidents connected with the increasing transport of chemicals and other hazardous substances became more prolific in the mid-1970s, with the London Fire Brigade responding to over 300 such incidents between Febuary 1973 and December 1975, which led the brigade to commission its own specialized chemical incident units.

These had trained crews and scientific advisers protected by gas-tight suits and breathing apparatus, and once they had been in contact with a dangerous substance, both the crew and their protective gear had to be cleaned and decontaminated, for which purpose units had 'dirty zones' in which the clothing was cleaned, either by vacuum cleaning or washing, while the crew was still wearing it. The crew then entered the vehicle to strip, shower and dress in

OPPOSITE: Land Rovers are also used as back-up rescue vehicles.

RIGHT: This Land Rover is used to ferry rescue workers to the scene.

PAGE 228: The Land Rover has a long heritage similar to that of the Jeep.

PAGE 229: Typical rescue equipment carried in a back-up vehicle.

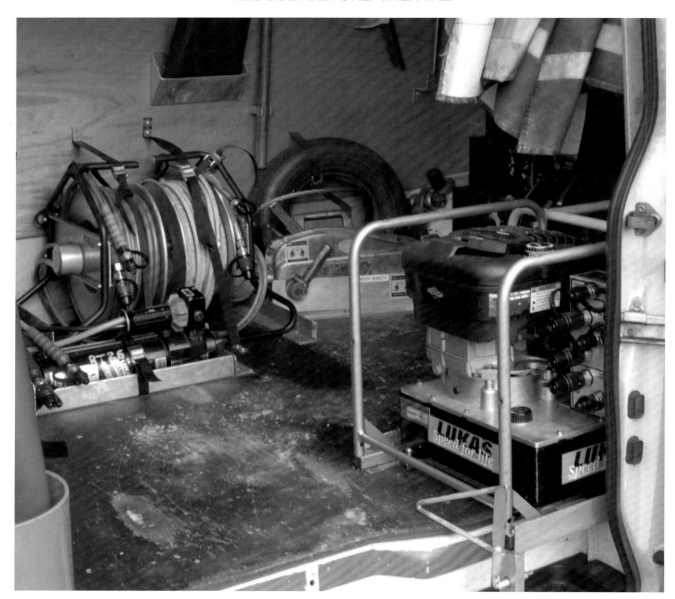

clean clothes before leaving this internal 'clean zone' by a different door.

Spilled or burning chemicals behave quite differently from conventional fires, and attacking them with water or foam may actually make matters worse. So the crew has to know exactly what they are facing and how to deal safely with the situation. One such example is the chemical incident unit supplied to the Royal Berkshire Fire & Rescue Service in 1994 which, along with full

OPPOSITE: A small generator, a shovel and cutting tools are also carried.

ABOVE: This Mercedes van is used to carry additional rescue equipment.

FIRE ENGINES

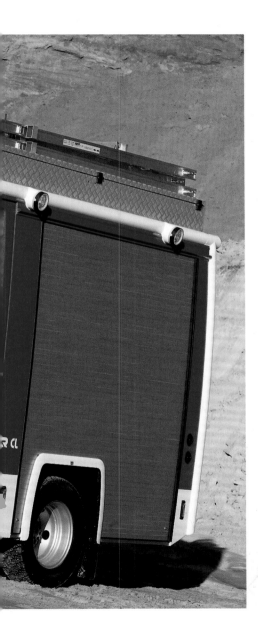

communication facilities (radio, cellnet fax and phone), had a computer which could access Chemdata, a database of over 20,000 substances, which detailed their dangers and how spills and fires involving them should be tackled. The vehicle also had other specialist equipment, such as a thermal imaging

LEFT: A fully-equipped back-up rescue vehicle.

BELOW: An IVECO-based conversion from Magirus.

camera and meters for detecting levels of oxygen and explosive mixtures present at the scene.

LEFT: A Mercedes rescue tender equipped with snow chains.

PAGE 236: By the look of the equipment, every kind of incident appears to be covered.

PAGE 237: These medium-duty rescue vehicles are popular in Europe.

E-One's HazMat appliance is also designed for just such incidents, based on both commercial and custom chassis and with a choice of body lengths from 18 to 24ft (0.45–0.6m). The specification encompasses many options, the most popular being HRT systems, a breathing air cascade system, lighting towers, generators (a choice of PTO, HY or petrol/diesel), shelves, trays and toolboards.

The HazMat is a specialist rescue vehicle, but more general-purpose units are based around Walk-In or Non-Walk-In formats, the one used depending on the specific needs of each fire department. The Walk-In is able to carry crew as well as equipment, and has space for a decontamination or command centre. The Non-Walk-In, apart from the cab, is devoted solely to carrying equipment. This choice is offered by several major manufacturers and some of them, such as Pierce, also

offer a Combination vehicle which includes elements of both.

E-One's Non-Walk-In is based on the custom Cyclone II or Typhoon chassis, and can seat up to eight crew in the cab. Everything rear of the cab is devoted to carrying equipment, and is festooned with compartments. Ultimate space depends on overall size, and E-One's NWI is offered with 16 to 22-ft (4.9–6.7-m) two-axle bodies or 24 and 26-ft three-axle bodies. Major options are a PTO-driven HRT, three, four or six-tool systems (all compatible with most hydraulic rescue tools), and various air-breathing systems (compressors, fill stations, air bottles, cascade systems), while engine-driven or self-powered diesel or petrol generators of 3.7– 5.6-hp (5–7.5kW) are also available.

The Walk-In offered by Pierce is typical of its kind, and again comes in two- or three-axle forms and with a whole range of body lengths from 14 to 26.5ft. It comes in three different heights and despite having less space than an equivalent Non-Walk-In, has a choice of around 50 different side-compartment arrangements. An

A medium-duty IVECO-based Magirus.

FIRE ENGINES

LEFT: A heavy-duty rescue vehicle from Sterling.

BELOW: Another from Bermuda.

PAGES 242–243: A very heavy rescue vehicle.

interesting feature is the recessed lighting tower, which has the benefits of protecting the tower from damage, lowering the rig's overall height, and producing a cleaner appearance. A smaller, more compact, option is a rescue vehicle based on a light pickup, such as the Classic FireRanger Rescue produced by E-One. Based on a Ford F550 four-wheel-drive chassis, this has an all-welded extruded-aluminium body, with roll-up doors and transverse compartments.

This is but a small selection of what was available in 2008, and to fully investigate all of the body permutations, the options of equipment, chassis and roles of modern rescue vehicles, would take a book in itself, which goes to show that the fire service today is concerned with rather more than merely fighting fires.

CARMICHAEL:
DIFFERENT BY DESIGN

*C*armichael claims to be the only UK manufacturer offering a full range of firefighting vehicles, having from the 1950s produced pumpers, turntable ladders, water tenders, hydraulic platforms and airport foam tenders. Until recently, these were based exclusively on British-built chassis from Dennis, Albion, Bedford, Land Rover, AEC, Leyland, Ford, Dodge and Commer, but imported chassis from IVECO, Timoney, Volvo and Scania have in recent times also been used.

Carmichael's Land Rover conversions were extensive, and the 1970 version was given a forward-control four-door cab that dramatically increased interior space, allowing it to carry not only a fire crew but also their equipment.

Two years later, the company launched its well-known 6x4 Range Rover, which involved lengthening the chassis of this world-famous luxury 4x4 and adding a third axle. The six-wheel Carmichael Range Rovers were favoured in the UK for dealing with motorway crashes, in that the 3.5-litre V8 petrol engine enabled it to get to accident scenes quickly, and to tow damaged vehicles off the road. It also came equipped with a front-mounted 200-gpm pump. The 6x4 was never mass-produced, and only 37 were delivered over seven years, but it was an effective showpiece for the whole company. More recently, Carmichael has offered an American General Motors pickup base as an alternative to the Land Rover.

Foremost among the company's current products are big airport crash tenders, an early example being the Cougar 8x8, based on an Irish Timoney chassis and delivered to the

British Airports Authority Fire Service in 1993. Powered by an 825-hp (615.2-kW) Detroit Diesel, this was capable of reaching 50mph (80km/h) in 32 seconds and delivering 1000gpm of foam from its roof-mounted monitor. The current Cobra 6x6 claims to have the biggest crewcab and doors (a metre wide) on the market, able to carry five firefighters, with equipment including a 3000-gallon water tank.

The UK market for fire engines is relatively small, and Carmichael exports around 70 per cent of its production, indicating that spreading the risk across different markets is a good recipe for survival.

GLOSSARY

Active Visual Warnings: Blue or red flashing lights, originally using a revolving mirror, then brighter strobe lights. LEDs are now increasingly being used.

Advance Life Support: Equipment to revive victims of cardiac arrest.

Audible Warnings: Bells have been replaced by sirens, and modern electronics produce a range of different sounds to suit the prevailing traffic conditions.

Backfiring: A tactic used in wildland firefighting, whereby firefighters intentionally set fire to fuels inside the control line, where they can choose the position. Often used to contain a rapidly spreading fire.

Backflow Preventer: A valve in hose fittings that allows water to flow in one direction only.

Barrel Strainer: A filter attachment for a hard-suction hose, designed to keep debris out of the water supply when drafting water from lakes or ponds.

Booster Line: The smallest hose on the engine of about 1-in (25-mm) diameter. Used on small wood fires or chimney fires.

Crash Tender: An airport fire engine capable of spraying foam.

Cross Lay: An arrangement that enables quick unloading of hoses from either side of a pumper. Also known as the Mattydale Lay.

Dead Lay: A hose not preconnected to a pump outlet; often used for larger hoses.

Deluge Gun: Also known as a deck gun, master stream or water cannon. A high-capacity water jet mounted high on the engine and able to deliver over 1000gpm of water onto large fires.

Draft Water Suction: Use of suction to move water from a tank, river, etc., through hoses. The pump creates a partial vacuum, and atmospheric pressure on water surface forces water into the pump.

Engine Pressure: Water pressure in a fire hose, measured at the pump outlet.

FAST (Firefighter Assist and Search Team): Also known as Rapid Entry Team or Rapid Intervention Team. Firefighters, who may have specialized training, experience and tools, and who stand by to rescue other firefighters.

Fires are classifed according to the elements involved, this being an aid to firefighting strategy. Classes are as follows:
 Class A: Involving ordinary combustibles, such as wood, paper or other natural materials.
 Class B: Involving flammable liquids, i.e., hydrocarbons such as petrol.
 Class C (Europe/Australia): involving flammable gases, e.g., petrolem vapour.
 Class C (USA): Involving electrical equipment.

FIRE ENGINES

Class D: Involving combustible metals, e.g., sodium, magnesium.

Class E (Europe/Australia): Involving electrical equipment.

Class F (Europe/Australia): involving cooking oils or fats.

Class K (USA): involving cooking oils or fats.

Fire Engine: Generic term for a firefighting vehicle, which may be multi-purpose or specialist.

Fire Hydrant: A water pipe, especially on a street, with a nozzle to which a fire hose can be attached. It accesses water mains in urban, suburban and occasionally rural areas.

Foam Concentrate: A raw foam liquid in a storage container, before it is mixed with water and air.

Foam Inductor: A specialized nozzle which mixes water and foam.

Forward Lay: Routing a fire hose from the water source towards the fire (opposite of Reverse Lay).

Friction Loss: Reduced water flow in a fire hose caused by friction between the water and the hose lining. The amount of friction loss depends primarily on diameter, type and length of hose, and the amount of water flowing through it.

GPM (gallons per minute): The standard measurement for the amount of water delivered by pumps/hoses/monitors.

Head Pressure: The standard measure of the pressure of water flow, based on a 1-inch (25-mm) hose and fixed nozzle. It records the 'breakover' point, when a water stream directed vertically breaks up and starts to fall back to the ground. If a stream breaks at 30ft, then the pump has 30ft of head pressure.

High Pressure System: An extra pump used to pressurize the water supply, used when more than one hydrant is delivering water, or during a large fire.

Hose Bed: The storage area for hoses on the fire engine.

Hydraulic platform: An aerial work platform, mounted on an articulated hydraulic boom, which can bend in one or more places to negotiate obstacles and be stowed for travel. It may be fitted with an emergency ladder, or be remotely-controlled in the case of dangerous chemical fires.

Impulse Fire Extinguishing System (IFEX): Water sprayed under very high pressure to form a mist, which cools the atmosphere, this being more effective than water alone.

Jaws of Life: An hydraulic rescue tool capable of prising or cutting open metalwork, often used at the sites of car crashes.

Jet Dump: This discharges all water as quickly as possible from the engine's tank into a drop tank.

Live Line: A fire hose under pressure from a pump, or a live electrical line that constitutes a hazard.

GLOSSARY

Logistical Support Appliances: Also known as 'hook loaders', which are able to carry a variety of specialist containers, depending on need, e.g., an oil destruction container, extra hoses, command centre, etc.

London Fire Brigade: The third largest in the world, with nearly 7,000 staff, and one of the busiest fire services in existence.

Midship: A ladder mounted directly behind the cab to allow a shorter wheelbase. Also the mounting of a water pump in the middle of the chassis.

Mobile Data Terminal: A wireless connection to a central computer, enabling firefighters to download maps, incident histories, etc., while on the emergency site.

Monitor: A water or foam jet, mounted on the roof of a fire engine, or on an aerial platform or ladder.

New York City Fire Dept. (FDNY): The biggest municipal fire service in the world, with over 14,000 uniformed staff, over 200 engines, and 142 trucks.

Paramedic Engine: A fast-response unit carrying firefighters and paramedics, capable of reaching emergency sites more quickly than a standard engine.

Passive Visual Warnings: Retro-reflective stickers, often checkerboard patterns or chevrons, that maximize the fire engine's visibility.

Plug: A slang term for fire hydrant, hydrants being at one time literally plugs in the tops of water mains.

Pump Escape: A fire engine carrying a wheeled ladder.

Pump Operator: A firefighter responsible for operating the pumps on a pumper, and who often drives the pumper as well.

Pumper: A fire engine with a water tank and pump.

Preconnects: Preconnected hoses, that save time on site, and which are usually 1.5- to 2.5-in (38–63.5-mm) diameter/250gpm.

Puncture Nozzle: A specialized tool that can puncture the skin of an aircraft or a wall to fight the fire within.

Quint (Quintuplet): A multi-purpose fire engine with five added features, e.g., pump, water tank, hoses, aerial device, ladders. The Quad (Quadruplet) has four features.

Ramming Pads: Rubberized pads on the fire engine's bodywork, enabling it to push stranded vehicles out of the way or act as a battering ram.

Rescue Pumper: A specialized engine developed by FDNY for rescue jobs. It has a 500-gallon tank but less hose than a standard engine, plus specialized rescue equipment.

Rescue Unit: This has been well-described as a large toolbox on wheels, carrying all the equipment needed in specialist situations, such as in car crashes or in rescues from water.

Reverse Lay: The fire hose is routed from the fire towards the water source, this being the opposite of Forward Lay.

Tailboard: The area at the rear of a fire engine, where fire fighters would once have ridden, standing up, in a dangerous practice now superseded by seated cabs. It can also be a step up to access hoses in a hose bed.

Tiller Truck: An articulated engine with rear-wheel steering to enable access to narrow streets.

Tower Ladder: A ladder with a basket or platform at the top, able to carry more than one person in rescues, and act as a secure base for firefighters.

Turntable Ladder: Also known as an Aerial Ladder, this being a long ladder mounted on a turntable on a truck chassis. The ladder is extended by means of hydraulics or pneumatics.

Twin Agent Fire Extinguisher System (TAFES): Delivers both dry chemical and foam. Dry chemical knocks the fire back, and foam leaves a blanket layer that smothers it and prevents re-ignition.

Utility Truck: A smaller truck used for incidents other than fires, such as repairs to water mains.

Water Tender/Tanker: A truck capable of transporting large quantities of water to the scene of a fire. Sometimes used to pump out floods. Most carry over 18,180 gallons (4000 litres), or 90,910 gallons (20000 litres) or more with a trailer.

Wet Down Ceremony: The 'christening' of a new fire engine by wetting it down before parking it in the station and adding mascots, bells, etc.

Wildfire: Also known as wildland fire, in forests, prairies, fields, commons, woods and other such uninhabited areas.

Wildland Fire Engines: Specialized engines used to combat wildfires. They may have a smaller water capacity than a standard engine, together with high ground clearance and the ability to climb mountain roads or drive off-road.

Wye: A Y-piece used as a hose junction to split a large supply hose into two smaller ones. A gated Wye includes valves so that certain lines can be turned on or off.

INDEX

INDEX